Snackable Bakes

100 Easy-Peasy Recipes for Exceptionally
Scrumptious Sweets and Treats

Jessie Sheehan

Countryman Press

An Imprint of W. W. Norton & Company
Independent Publishers Since 1923

Copyright © 2022 by Jessie Sheehan
Photographs copyright © 2022 by Nico Schinco

All rights reserved
Printed in the United States of America

For information about permission to reproduce selections from this book,
write to Permissions, Countryman Press, 500 Fifth Avenue, New York, NY 10110

For information about special discounts for bulk purchases, please contact
W. W. Norton Special Sales at specialsales@wwnorton.com or 800-233-4830

Manufacturing by Versa Press
Book design by Allison Chi
Production manager: Devon Zahn

Countryman Press
www.countrymanpress.com

An imprint of W. W. Norton & Company, Inc.
500 Fifth Avenue, New York, NY 10110
www.wwnorton.com

978-1-68268-737-6

10 9 8 7 6 5 4 3 2 1

To my parents, for putting dessert on the table every night of the week (aka, for raising me right), and to Matt, for just about everything else.

Contents

Introduction

What Is a Snackable Bake?

I know what you're thinking (because, yes, I'm not only the queen of easy-peasy baking, but I'm also a mind reader), "What on earth is a *snackable bake* and is it possible to get one in my belly right now?!" Well, a snackable bake is an utterly scrumptious, round-the-clock treat that is quick and easy to assemble, requires limited equipment, and satisfies a sweets craving whenever it hits. And, yes, it *is* possible to enjoy such a bake sooner rather than later, because typically a snackable bake satiates the abovementioned craving in an hour or less. Oh, and to be clear, I'm using the word "bakes" loosely here, as this book includes *all kinds* of snackable treats, but not every one of them requires an oven (you're welcome).

Why I Love Snackable Bakes and Why You Should, Too

I adore snackable bakes due to my voracious sweet tooth and my impatient nature. I dig making and eating from-scratch goodies on the regular, but I'm not super fond of kitchen "projects" (croissants, layer cakes, even pie dough, I'm looking at you). I like sweets and treats with short, pantry-staple ingredient lists (a snackable baker like myself isn't crazy about run-

ning to multiple grocery stores in order to make cookies) and straightforward, unambiguous instructions. I like assembling recipes using a bowl or two, a whisk, and a flexible spatula (in addition to being a "snackable baker," I will also answer to "one-bowl baker"). And I *love* measuring ingredients with a scale when I bake because it means less cleanup—and I won't lie: I despise cleanup.

Any chance this sounds a little like you? Oh, yay! I was hoping you'd say that, as this book of 100 recipes for utterly mouthwatering snackable bakes is 100 percent for you. But you know what? Even if your idea of a good time is making a dessert that requires six different components be assembled over a 72-hour period, this book *still* deserves a place on your shelf. Because here's the thing: *Snackable Bakes* is for *everyone* who has a soft (and sweet) spot for making and eating delicious treats, such as Butter Cracker Toffee Bark with Toasted Nuts (page 190), Deeply Chocolaty Baked Donuts with Buttermilk Glaze and Sprinkles (page 91), Brown Sugar Fruit Slump (page 39), Banana Snacking Cake with Chocolate Malted Cream Cheese Frosting (page 50), and Peppermint Stick No-Churn Ice Cream Sundaes (page 163). In other words, whether you identify as a snackable baker or not, if you like icebox cakes and buckles, puddings and snacking cakes, fudge and blondies, mousse and tiramisu, cookies and bark, there is something delightfully toothsome in here for you, too.

How I Came to Be a Snackable Baker

Although it's fair to say that I'm now the snackable bakes team captain, I didn't even begin as a team *member*—or baker, for that matter. I mean, my love of sweets goes way back, but it was a love born of Double Stuf Oreos, Drake's Devil Dogs, and Entenmann's chocolate chip cookies, with slices of Sarah Lee pound cake and a few Pepperidge Farm Mint Milanos thrown in for good measure. There wasn't much baking from scratch happening in my childhood home, so there were no lessons learned at an apron-clad family member's side, and my first word was decidedly not "whisk." Moreover, there was acting and lawyering and mothering going on before there was *ever* baking.

And, funnily enough, when the baking first began, merely as a way to ensure that the sweets and treats I was purchasing and eating anyway were always on hand and in (relative) bulk), it wasn't of the simple, snackable variety. Instead, because I hadn't yet been bit by the easy-peasy bug, I was as ready as the next person to pull out my stand mixer for *every* recipe I tackled; to run to the store to search out special flours and sweeteners and unusual herbs and spices; to embrace delayed satisfaction when a cookie needed a 72-hour rest and a pie dough to be chilled overnight and then frozen prebake; and to prepare a birthday cake for one of my young boys that required not only three chocolate layers and a whipped ganache frosting, but also a flavored simple-syrup soak, and a from-scratch caramel filling (and don't even get me started on the mandatory piping of the "Happy Birthday," which was—and still is—a struggle).

But after a while, my enthusiasm waned for the aforementioned, drawn-out, multiple-stepped,

project-like recipes, and as I flipped through the pages of *Living, Cook's Illustrated,* and *Fine Cooking,* magazines gifted to me by my mother-in-law (see page 46 for more on my MIL and her mags), as well as those of my favorite baking cookbooks by Martha Stewart, Dorie Greenspan, Shirley Corriher, and the smarties at King Arthur Baking Company, as well as others (yes, peeps, this was the olden days, before the internet was everyone's favorite recipe source), it was the recipes for sweets and baked goods that all fit on one page, with an ingredient list no longer than a column—preferably less—and with instructions that did not include "In the bowl of a stand mixer..." that I dog-eared. They were for candies that didn't require thermometers, donuts that didn't require frying, cinnamon buns that didn't require yeast, and cakes of a single layer with a simple glaze or buttercream (aka snacking cakes). In short, my lovely readers, an obsession with unfussy baking was born. I gravitated toward such recipes at home, when satisfying my own cravings or celebrating my then-toddler sons' milestones (like the fact that we'd all made it to Tuesday), but also professionally, as I started exclusively pitching and developing easy baking recipes, with all of the previously mentioned attributes of a snackable bake, to the different magazines, newspapers, and food sites to which I contribute. And, honestly, the rest is history (in the form of this cookbook).

Snackable Baking Is Having a Moment

As it turned out, I am not the only one with a fondness for uncomplicated treats. My fellow food folks now throw around the words "one-bowl," "simple," and "fast" with absolute abandon when describing sweets recipes for everything from ice cream to galettes to coffee cakes to meringues (for the record, I don't *personally* believe meringues belong in an "effortless baking" category, due to the egg white whipping that they require, but I'm trying not to be too judge-y). I mean, snackable baking is legit having a moment and I couldn't be more excited to celebrate that with this cookbook—an easy-peasy sweets book full of recipes that:

- **can all be assembled in about 20 minutes or less**;
- **will never require you to cream softened butter, rest cookie dough, chill/freeze pie dough, or perform any other time-sucking task** (all of which *of course* have their place, but just not in a baking book such as this one);
- **will never require you to whisk egg whites in a stand mixer** and **will only require you to separate them, like, once or twice** (I know, you're not happy, but once you've tried my ultra-creamy Individual Butterscotch Puddings [page 180], you'll be grateful the recipe called only for yolks and thrilled that the extra whites mean that that batch of the Straight-Up Coconut Macaroons [page 124] you've been eyeing might just be happening, stat);
- **will rarely require that you pull out your stand mixer (or hand mixer)** except when making frosting or whipped cream, and yes, the best no-bake cheesecake you've ever had;
- *might* **require you to pull out your food processor**—like once, but only so you can make the epic citrus filling for the No-Bake Orange Cream Pie with a Pretzel Crust (page 186); and
- *will* **strongly suggest that you melt butter and chocolate in your microwave** (if you have one)—sorry, haters.

And on the off chance you're wondering, "What, with all this stuff that I *won't* be doing when snackable baking, how will these sweets and treats compare to the ones I'm used to?" To put it simply, they will knock your socks off. I mean, maybe you think that that flourless chocolate cake of yours where you separate the eggs and whisk the whites till peaky in your stand mixer and the yolks till ribbony with your hand mixer is the best you've ever had, but that's only because you've never had mine (page 98). It's assembled in a single bowl, requires whole eggs, takes about 3 minutes to throw together and about 30 minutes to bake, and is just gorgeous (to look at and to eat). Yes, of course, cakes with rye or buckwheat flour, muffins with passion fruit, cookies that rest for three days, scones that you freeze prebake, and grinding and toasting your own spices for your pumpkin cake *do* make for elevated sweets, but here's the thing: elevated doesn't *always* mean better.

The Snackable Baker's Ingredients, Tools, Tips, and Techniques

Ingredients

If you have a sweet tooth, or are even sweet tooth adjacent, and bake on occasion, you likely have all the ingredients you need to make almost every recipe in this book in your kitchen right now. These are "pantry-friendly" recipes *by design*, as I want you to be able to open the book, point to a recipe that you'd like to enjoy ASAP, and make it right then and there.

Pantry-Friendly

In my pantry, and, ideally, in yours, too, I always have:

- UNBLEACHED ALL-PURPOSE FLOUR—If you only have bleached, no worries, that'll work, too.
- GRANULATED, LIGHT BROWN, AND CON- FECTIONERS' SUGAR—I usually have dark brown on hand, too, just sayin'.
- DUTCH-PROCESSED COCOA POWDER—I love it for its dark color and deep chocolate flavor, and all the recipes in this book were developed using it, but if you only have nat- ural cocoa on hand, that's a-okay.
- CHOCOLATE CHIPS—Chips are basically my love language, as they are easier to measure (volume-wise) than bar choc- olate and chopping is rarely involved when using them (i.e., no knife, no cutting board, no time spent doing so), and this is, after all, a book that celebrates simplified baking. On the *rare* occasion that a rec- ipe benefits from chocolate smaller than a chip, I will ask you to chop your chips (as I'm loathe to ask you to go purchase minis . . .), and if this happens, take a deep breath and grab a serrated knife—it'll make chopping those pesky little bits that are just jonesing to jump off your cutting board a little easier.
- NONSTICK COOKING SPRAY—Of course, you can grease with softened butter if you'd like, but I started using spray back in my bakery days and have never looked back. I mean, can you say "convenient"?!
- KOSHER SALT—Fine sea salt will work, too, but I'm a kosher gal, and my preferred brand is Diamond Crystal.

- VEGETABLE OIL—I call for vegetable oil in this book, even though I often reach for a mild olive oil when I bake at home. Either will work.
- LARGE EGGS—When baking, egg size mat- ters (sorry, but it's true). Using extra-large eggs in a recipe calling for large, for exam- ple, can make brownies cakey and cookie dough too wet, or the cookies themselves too fluffy. If you can swing it, go large or go home, is all I'm sayin'.
- MILK, HEAVY CREAM, BUTTERMILK—You may not have all three, I get it. But if a recipe calls for buttermilk and you've got either milk or cream, you can make DIY buttermilk by adding 1 tablespoon of freshly squeezed lemon juice or vinegar to 1 cup (237 ml) of milk or cream (or even nondairy milk). Let sit for about 5 minutes until slightly curdled and use as you would buttermilk.
- FULL-FAT SOUR CREAM AND/OR WHOLE- MILK YOGURT—Yup, they're always around, and I mean, yes, you *can* use low-fat, but why would you?
- VANILLA EXTRACT—Fun fact: I am *extremely* vanilla-forward and use vanilla with abandon . . . scale back if this freaks you out.
- LEMONS—They don't *always* make their way into a bake of mine, but with fruity desserts, a squeeze of juice is often called for—plus a couple of squeezes will firm up a no-bake cheesecake like nobody's business.
- NUTS (WALNUTS, PECANS, HAZELNUTS)—I usually have a variety and I like them raw and unsalted. Oh, and I like to freeze them so they stay fresh indefinitely(ish).

Pantry-Companionable (Not "Friends" with My Pantry Per Se, but Most Definitely Warmly Acquainted)

Although *I* always have the following items in my pantry, as well as the ones listed previously, you may not, and you might want to consider stocking up—that is, if building a snackable bakes ingredient arsenal sounds fun to you (and I'm obvs hoping it sounds like the best time ever).

- **CAKE FLOUR**—It is only required when making my Extra Crumb Snacking Cake (page 65), but since you're likely to become obsessed with making said cake, maybe you can bite the bullet and purchase a box? But if not, make your own: whisk 14 tablespoons (114 g) of all-purpose flour (1 cup minus 2 tablespoons) with 2 tablespoons of cornstarch and then sift the mixture twice before using.

- **SELF-RISING FLOUR**—Again, it's only called for once, when making my Rhubarb Cobbler with Easy-Peasy Biscuits (page 36) and, again, you can DIY it (you lucky devil). For every cup of self-rising flour, whisk 1 cup (130 g) all-purpose flour with 1½ teaspoons of baking powder and ¼ teaspoon of kosher salt.

- **TURBINADO SUGAR (SUCH AS SUGAR IN THE RAW)**—I turn to it constantly when adding texture and sparkle to the tops of scones, muffins, and cakes.

- **SWEETENED CONDENSED MILK**—This is basically my favorite ingredient, and essential when making no-churn ice cream (pages 163, 164, and 167), or preparing Secret Ingredient Crispy Rice Cereal Treats (page 73), or indulging in Coconut Tres Leches Snacking Cake (page 150), which also calls for evap-orated milk, coconut milk, and sweetened coconut cream—I know: I'm the worst, but trust me: the cake is *fab*.

- **CREAM CHEESE**—'Cause, well, cream cheese.

- **NUT FLOURS**—I usually have bags of almond and hazelnut flours in my freezer and you will need both for a couple of the recipes herein. Place the bags in your freezer, well sealed, and they will last at least until you decide you want to remake Almond Sandwich Cookies with Jam Buttercream (page 182) and Hazelnut Chip Snacking Cake with Chocolate Hazelnut Whipped Cream (page 136), which will likely be sooner than you think. Hazelnut flour can be a little trickier to track down than almond, so to make 1 cup at home, process about ¾ cup (107 g) of whole hazelnuts in your food processer until finely ground.

- **ESPRESSO POWDER**—I don't call for it to make things taste like coffee, except in the case of Oliver's Simplest Tiramisu (page 168) but because it pops the flavor of chocolate (yup, it's true). It's always optional, however, so no pressure.

- **CULINARY GRADE DRIED LAVENDER**—Okay, you're right: I don't *always* have dried lavender in the pantry, but I do love it in my Tiny Lavender Shortbread Bites (page 205), and thinking you might, too.

- **CRÈME FRAÎCHE**—I've a weakness for it, I won't lie, and it is fab in my Chocolate Crème Fraîche Banana Bread (page 88), but sub sour cream if you want: I'm totes cool with that.

- **FOOD COLORING**—I know it's not everyone's favorite, but I dig a little drop here or a little drop there to brighten things up—I mean, a little pop of color is never a bad thing, am I right?

- **FREEZE-DRIED STRAWBERRIES**—Honestly, it's just my Strawberry-n-Cream Bar Cookies (page 74) that call for them, but they last a while and are easily found at most grocery stores. And if strawberry whipped cream sounds like something you might like, try whisking ½ cup (13 g) of ground dehydrated strawberries and a tablespoon or two of confectioners' sugar into every cup (236 ml) of heavy cream before whipping . . . YUM.

Tools

You can literally assemble almost every recipe in this book with nothing more than a whisk and a bowl. *However*, there are a few kitchen items of which I am particularly fond and so wanted to share.

- **HEATPROOF FLEXIBLE SPATULA**—Helpful for gently folding flour into wet ingredients and for scraping batter into pans—and also for gently stirring chocolate as it melts in a pan on the stovetop.
- **WHISK**—Great for whisking wet ingredients, and in a pinch, also not bad for mixing the wet into the dry—just needs to be done with a light hand.
- **BENCH SCRAPER (FOR CUBING BUTTER)**—I mean, it's a little obscure, I get it, but since we're talking tools, I thought it worth mentioning.
- **LONG WOODEN SKEWERS (FOR TESTING BAKED GOODS FOR DONENESS)**—Sometimes toothpicks are just too short and too smooth.
- **PORTION SCOOPS (FOR PORTIONING COOKIES AND SCONES AND MUFFINS AND . . . BASICALLY EVERYTHING)**—So helpful for accuracy. Also, scooping = less-mess-making. I recommend three

sizes: 1½ tablespoons, 2 tablespoons, and ¼ cup.

- **FOOD PROCESSER**—Not *necessary* per se, but if you have one, please use it to make the filling for my No-Bake Orange Cream Pie with a Pretzel Crust (page 186). It's also fantastic for turning cookies into crumbs for crusts and butter into pea-sized bits for bars, buns, scones, and tortes.
- **STAND MIXER**—Yes, for whipped cream/icebox cakes, no-churn ice creams, no-bake cheesecake, and frostings you will want to use one, but it goes without saying that you can *always* use a hand mixer instead (I won't repeat that fact in every recipe, but I think you'll remember . . .).
- **BAKING PANS**—You will need an 8-inch square and an 8-inch round cake pan, a 9-inch round cake pan, an 8½-by-4½-inch loaf pan, a 9-by-13-inch baking pan, a springform pan for the (epically yum) Vanilla No-Bake Cheesecake with a Chocolate Cookie Crust (page 82), a 9½-inch tart pan with a removable bottom for the Dreamiest Peanut Butter Chocolate Cup (page 140), and standard-sized rimmed baking sheets—for cookies, scones, brittle, bark, and more.
- **PARCHMENT PAPER**—'Nuf said.

Tips and Techniques

A few simple baking tips and techniques for your snackable baking pleasure:

HOW TO STREAMLINE THE ASSEMBLY OF YOUR BAKES: Rather than mix your dry ingredients and wet ingredients separately in two different bowls, as baking recipes traditionally call for, vigorously whisk the leavening, salt, and spices—one at a time—*directly into* the wet ingredients; and once combined, *then* fold in the flour. Typi-

cally, when folding the dry ingredients into the wet, there is a tendency to overmix, in an effort to ensure that the baking powder and soda are thoroughly combined. Sadly, though, such thoroughness unintentionally produces tough, dry treats. This brilliant, timesaving technique not only avoids all that, as it effectively prevents you from overworking your flour and produces tender baked goods every time, but it also precludes the dirtying of multiple bowls (which the one-bowl baker in me just loves). It was introduced to me by my pal Deb Perelman (the genius behind Smitten Kitchen) and, honestly, I have never looked back.

HOW TO TOAST NUTS AND COCONUT: Heat the oven to 350°F and evenly spread the nuts/coconut on a baking sheet. Bake until lightly browned and fragrant, 10 to 15 minutes, stirring occasionally.

HOW TO BRING EGGS TO ROOM TEMP QUICKLY: Place the whole eggs (still in their shell) in a small bowl of hot tap water for about 5 minutes.

HOW TO MELT BUTTER AND CHOCOLATE ON THE STOVETOP: If I've said it once, I've said it a billion times: I am very microwave-forward and use mine with abandon when melting butter and chocolate. But if you do not have a microwave or are just generally less excited about yours than I am about mine, you do you, and use the stovetop. Melt butter in a small saucepan over low heat and chocolate in a heatproof bowl nestled atop a pot that contains an inch or so of simmering water (but don't let the bottom of the bowl touch the water). Although I won't mention these techniques in every recipe, just know that I support you in all of your stovetop melting endeavors.

HOW TO MELT *AND COOL* BUTTER AND CHOCOLATE *SIMULTANEOUSLY:* Sounds a little funny, I know, but often recipes require butter or chocolate to be melted, but also *cooled*. To achieve this, melt only until *most* of the butter/chocolate has liquefied, but some solid bits remain; then whisk by hand until smooth.

And finally, a note about **how long (or not long) it is going to take you to make the recipes in this book**: Yes, it's true—every recipe can be assembled in about 20 minutes or less, but some sweets will take longer to bake than others—and when I say longer, I mean like over an hour (Blackberry Lemon Yogurt Loaf Cake [page 23] and Raspberry Crumb-Topped Pie with Easiest Ever Crust and Crumble [page 40], we are all looking at you)—and some will need time to set up, sometimes overnight. And that is not cool; I get it. But that is also life, and I promise you can do whatever it is you want while those yummy treats bake or rest or chill in the fridge, like binge-watch an excellent TV show (I know of *many*, so DM me for a list).

How to Use This Book

The snackable bakes in this book are organized by flavor (vanilla, chocolate, fruity, spicy, etc.), but if you just *know* you want to make a cake (or a cookie or a confection), head right over to the index (page 236), where you will find all the snackable bakes organized by type. And note well: many of the recipes have variations—so you can make a vanilla cheesecake, *as well as* a lemon one, jam-filled "rebel" bars *and* chocolate-filled ones, cherry vanilla muffins *alongside* raspberry lemon ones—in short, it's a veritable *flavor party* and I'm so glad you're one of the guests.

CHAPTER 1. Fruit Forward

Fruit for the win always, am I right? I mean, yes, yes, yes: I love *all* the snackable bakes and *all* are utterly delish, fruity or not. But juicy berries in muffins and loaf cakes, and toothsome chunks of apple in pie bars, and tart cherries in a dreamy custardy clafoutis, and lemon juice in a posset (pudding's cute little cousin) can't be beat. And many believe there is something slightly more virtuous about indulging in a fruit-filled sweet, rather than one that is not. Or that if a treat includes fruit, then it clearly belongs at the breakfast table. I personally believe there is virtue in all the bakes (and that they are all appropriate at any time of day—I mean, everything in moderation, right?). But I'm here for the fruit-love, no matter the form it takes. Now, sadly, you will not be able to find *all* of these different fruits in your local grocery *all* the time, due to seasonality and all that. However, I am a big fan of frozen fruit: either your own—stored in a resealable plastic bag and tucked away in the back of your freezer (don't forget it's there!)—or packaged from the store. And, often, frozen is—miraculously—just as tasty. No need to defrost first when using it, but you will likely need to add a few minutes to your baking time, as the frozen berries or chunks of peach or rhubarb cool the batter, and—fun fact—a chillier batter requires a longer bake time. Finally, it goes without saying that *Extremely* Special Whipped Cream (page 230) and vanilla ice cream are fruit-forward snackable bakes' besties. So, keep that top of mind when serving up a slice of Matt's Blueberry Galette (page 43) or a Better-Than-Apple-Pie Bar (page 32) or a heaping helping of Brown Sugar Fruit Slump (page 39) or Rhubarb Cobbler with Easy-Peasy Biscuits (page 36). But don't fret if you don't have either on hand: in a pinch, a drizzle of heavy cream is really all you need.

Not Your Grandma's Blueberry Streusel Muffins

MAKES 15 MUFFINS
ACTIVE TIME: 10 MINUTES
BAKE TIME: 25 TO 30 MINUTES

FOR THE STREUSEL

½ cup (100 g) granulated sugar
½ cup (65 g) all-purpose flour
¼ teaspoon kosher salt
¼ cup (56 g) unsalted butter, cold and cubed

FOR THE MUFFINS

⅓ cup (79 ml) vegetable oil
1⅓ cups (267 g) granulated sugar
2 teaspoons vanilla extract
2 large eggs
½ cup (118 ml) buttermilk
1½ teaspoons baking powder
¼ teaspoon baking soda
½ teaspoon kosher salt
2 cups (260 g) all-purpose flour
2 cups (280 g) blueberries, fresh or frozen

VARIATION

For Not Your Grandma's Sparkly Blueberry Muffins, omit the streusel and generously sprinkle the muffin tops with turbinado sugar before baking.

Okay, I'm joking—maybe these were *your* grandmother's muffins. They just weren't mine, and boy, do I wish they had been. Everyone appreciates (or at least everyone with whom I hang) a classic fluffy and tender blueberry muffin, and if it's topped with streusel, well then, all the better. You can totes use frozen berries here, but they may bleed a little and turn your muffins green(ish). To avoid this, rinse the berries till the water runs clean and then dry them before using. Yes, this is a tiny bit fussy, but only a *teeny* tiny bit.

1. Heat the oven to 400°F. Line a 12-well muffin tin with paper liners.

2. To make the streusel, whisk together the sugar, flour, and salt in a medium bowl. Rub in the butter, using your fingers, until the mixture holds together when squeezed. Refrigerate the streusel while you make the muffins.

3. To make the muffins, whisk together the oil, sugar, and vanilla in a large bowl for 30 seconds. Whisk in the eggs, one at a time, and then the buttermilk. Sprinkle the baking powder, baking soda, and salt into the bowl, one at a time, whisking vigorously after each. Gently fold in the flour just until a few streaks of flour remain. Fold in the blueberries. Don't overmix.

4. Fill each prepared muffin well about three-quarters full, using a spoon or a ¼-cup portion scoop, and sprinkle the muffins with the chilled streusel, lightly pressing it into the batter with your hands. Bake for 25 to 30 minutes. At the halfway point, lower the oven temperature to 350°F and rotate the tin. The muffins are done when a wooden skewer inserted into the center of one comes out with only a moist crumb or two and the streusel is just starting to brown. Remove from the oven and let cool about 5 minutes, or until you can safely remove the muffins from the tin without burning yourself. Repeat with the remaining batter and streusel, rinsing the pan in cold water to cool it, drying and relining it between rounds. Serve warm or at room temperature. Keep the muffins in an airtight container on the counter for up to 3 days.

Blackberry Lemon Yogurt Loaf Cake

MAKES ONE 8½-BY-4½-INCH
LOAF CAKE
ACTIVE TIME: 10 MINUTES
BAKE TIME: 60 TO 70 MINUTES

Cooking spray or softened
   unsalted butter for pan
2 tablespoons lemon zest, from
   about 2 lemons
1 cup (200 g) granulated sugar
½ cup (118 ml) vegetable oil
¾ teaspoon vanilla extract
2 large eggs, at room
   temperature
2 tablespoons freshly squeezed
   lemon juice
½ cup (120 g) whole-milk yogurt,
   at room temperature
2 teaspoons baking powder
¼ teaspoon kosher salt
1½ cups (195 g) all-purpose flour
1½ cups (195 g) blackberries, fresh
   or frozen, roughly chopped
Turbinado sugar for sprinkling

VARIATIONS

For Blueberry Lemon Yogurt
Loaf Cake, substitute blueberries for the blackberries—
no need to chop them. For
Cherry Almond Yogurt Loaf
Cake, substitute quartered
cherries—sour or sweet—for
the blackberries. Omit the zest
and juice; reduce the vanilla
to ½ teaspoon and add ¾ teaspoon of almond extract.

I won't lie, this was *the* most challenging recipe in the book to get right (and by "right" I mean *perfect*) and that means that, yes, I had no fewer than six different lovelies test it for me. The cake itself owes a little something to Dorie Greenspan and to Ina Garten (I like giving credit where credit is due). It is a sensationally moist and flavorful cake, and the chopped berries release their juices while baking, creating little juicy berry pockets (yes, berry pockets are a thing). The cake is nothing short of summer in a loaf pan.

1. Heat the oven to 350°F. Grease an 8½-by-4½-inch loaf pan with cooking spray or softened butter. Line the bottom with a long sheet of parchment paper that extends up and over the long sides of the pan (like a cradle for your cake).

2. Rub the lemon zest into the granulated sugar with your fingers in a large bowl until fragrant. Whisk in the oil and vanilla for 30 seconds. Whisk in the eggs, one at a time, and then the lemon juice and yogurt. Sprinkle the baking powder and salt into the bowl, one at a time, vigorously whisking after each. Gently fold in the flour just until a few streaks remain. Fold in 1 cup (130 g) of the berries. The batter will be lumpy.

3. Scrape the batter into the prepared pan, smooth the top, and arrange the remaining ½ cup of berries over the top of the loaf. Lightly sprinkle with turbinado sugar and bake for 60 to 70 minutes, rotating at the halfway point. The cake is done when a wooden skewer inserted into the center comes out with a moist crumb or two. Remove from the oven and let cool in the pan for about 20 minutes, or until you can safely lift the cake out by the parchment overhang without burning yourself. Run a butter knife around the edges if it resists. Let cool to room temperature before slicing and serving. Keep the cake, wrapped, on the counter for up to 3 days.

Sour Cherry Clafoutis

MAKES ABOUT 9 SERVINGS
ACTIVE TIME: 5 MINUTES
BAKING TIME: 35 TO 40 MINUTES

Cooking spray or softened
    unsalted butter for pan
1 pound (454 g) sour cherries,
    stemmed and pitted, or regu-
    lar cherries, fresh or frozen
2 tablespoons turbinado sugar,
    plus more for sprinkling
3 large eggs
2 teaspoons vanilla extract
¼ teaspoon almond extract
½ cup (100 g) granulated sugar
¼ teaspoon kosher salt
1½ cups (355 ml) half-and-half or
    whole milk
⅔ cup (87 g) all-purpose flour
Confectioners' sugar for dusting

A clafoutis is a quick (French!) wonder from way back. It is traditionally made with sweet cherries (but I love it with sour ones, if you can find them) baked up in a custard and served warm with maybe a dusting of confectioners' sugar. It takes about 5 minutes to assemble, is just lightly sweetened, and should become a card-carrying member of your recipe repertoire, stat. Substitute berries or even chopped stone fruit for the cherries, if you're feeling adventurous. Or embrace your inner rule-follower and source out some sour cherries, if in season.

1. Heat the oven to 350°F. Grease an 8-inch square cake pan or a 2-quart baking dish with cooking spray or softened butter.

2. Scatter the cherries over the bottom of the prepared pan. Evenly sprinkle the turbinado sugar over the cherries and toss to coat with your hands or a flexible spatula. Vigorously whisk together the eggs, extracts, granulated sugar, and salt in a large bowl for 30 seconds. Whisk in the half-and-half and then the flour until almost smooth. A few lumps are okay.

3. Pour the batter over the cherries and sprinkle the top with additional turbinado sugar. Bake for 35 to 40 minutes, until the top puffs up, the color is golden, and it is just set. Remove from the oven, let cool slightly (it will deflate), dust with confectioners' sugar, and serve. Keep the clafoutis, wrapped, in the refrigerator for up to 3 days.

Summer Peach Fritters

MAKES 20 FRITTERS
ACTIVE TIME: 5 MINUTES
FRYING TIME: 20 TO 30 MINUTES

Vegetable oil for frying, plus
  1 tablespoon for batter
1 cup (130 g) all-purpose flour
½ cup (56 g) cornstarch
¼ cup (50 g) granulated sugar
1¼ teaspoons baking powder
¾ teaspoon kosher salt
⅓ cup (79 ml) whole milk
1 large egg
1½ teaspoons vanilla extract
2 cups (280 g) cubed, unpeeled
  peaches (from about
  3 medium peaches)
Confectioners' sugar for dusting

VARIATION

For Cinnamon-Sugar
Apple Fritters, substitute
2 cups peeled and cubed
apples for the peaches.
Rather than dust the just-fried
fritters with confectioners'
sugar, toss them in cinnamon-
sugar: whisk together 1 cup
(200 g) of granulated sugar
and 1 tablespoon of ground
cinnamon with a fork in a
small, shallow bowl. Roll the
warm fritters in the mixture
before serving.

It's true: no one *loves* frying at home. Eating fried food at home? Yes. But frying it yourself? No, thanks. But hear me out. These adorbs little peach fritters can literally be assembled in the time it takes your oil to come to temp. And the peaches? You don't even need to skin them, just chop. Fritters are best served warm and will be happening so quickly, because the assembly is so speedy, that by the time you realize that maybe your cooktop is just a tad oil-splattered, you'll be popping warm fritters in your mouth with abandon and won't even care.

1. Line a cooling rack with a thick layer of paper towels and set near the cooktop. Fill a large heavy pot with 2 inches of oil. Attach a candy thermometer to the side of the pot and heat the oil over medium-high heat until the temperature reaches 350°F, or a bit above.

2. While the oil heats, whisk together the flour, cornstarch, granulated sugar, baking powder, and salt in a medium bowl. Whisk together the 1 tablespoon of oil, milk, egg, and vanilla in a large bowl for 30 seconds. Gently fold the dry ingredients into the wet with a flexible spatula until just a streak or two of flour remain. Fold in the peaches.

3. Carefully drop 1½ tablespoons of batter into the hot oil. Fry the fritters for about 3 minutes total, gently flipping them over with wooden chopsticks or a slotted spoon at the halfway point. Depending on the size of your pot and your patience level, you may fry one fritter at a time or up to five or six—but don't overcrowd the pot. Using a slotted spoon, carefully transfer the fritters to the prepared cooling rack. Dust with confectioners' sugar. Peach fritters are best enjoyed warm on the day they are made.

Pink Grapefruit Graham Bars

MAKES 16 BARS
ACTIVE TIME: 20 MINUTES
BAKE TIME: 35 MINUTES

Cooking spray or softened
   unsalted butter for pan

FOR THE CRUST
14 full graham crackers (220 g;
   about 2¼ cups ground)

3 tablespoons granulated sugar

½ teaspoon kosher salt

6 tablespoons (85 g) unsalted
   butter, melted and cooled
   slightly

FOR THE FILLING
One 14-ounce can (397 g) sweetened condensed milk

1 tablespoon pink grapefruit zest

¼ teaspoon kosher salt

½ cup (118 ml) freshly squeezed
   and *strained* pink grapefruit
   juice

2 tablespoons freshly squeezed
   lemon juice

3 large eggs

A drop or two of red food coloring (optional)

Confectioners' sugar for dusting

VARIATION

For Lemon Graham Bars,
substitute ½ cup (118 g) of freshly
squeezed and *strained* lemon
juice for the ½ cup of grapefruit
juice, omit the 2 tablespoons
of lemon juice, substitute
1 tablespoon of lemon zest for
the grapefruit zest, and omit
the food coloring.

These bars are "pink" in name only (unless you add a drop of red food coloring, which I highly encourage). But, hey, just because they swing a little more yellowy/orange than not doesn't mean they don't have a wonderfully tart, citrus flavor, and a creamy texture (from the love of my sweets-making life, sweetened condensed milk) that marries beautifully with the buttery, crispy graham. They've got all that, and then some.

1. Heat the oven to 350°F. Grease an 8-inch square cake pan with cooking spray or softened butter. Line with a long piece of parchment paper that extends up and over two opposite sides of the pan.

2. To make the crust, process the crackers, granulated sugar, and salt in the bowl of a food processor until the crackers are finely ground. Pour in the melted butter and process until the mixture holds together when squeezed. Alternatively, you may seal the dry ingredients in a resealable plastic bag, cover it with a tea towel, crush the crackers with a rolling pin, then transfer the crumbs to a medium bowl, and stir in the butter. Scrape the mixture into the prepared pan and firmly press it into the bottom. Bake the crust for 16 to 18 minutes, until golden brown, rotating at the halfway point. Lower the oven temperature to 325°F.

3. Meanwhile, to make the filling, combine all its ingredients, except the eggs and food coloring (if using), in a large bowl and whisk until smooth. Gently whisk in the eggs and then a drop or two of food coloring (if using). Carefully press down on the edges of the hot crust with the bottom of a 1-cup dry measuring cup (this step adheres the crust to the bottom of the pan and precludes the filling seeping underneath it), pour in the filling, and bake for about 17 minutes, or until the filling has set but still jiggles just slightly in the center. Remove from the oven, let cool to room temperature, and then refrigerate until cold, about 2 hours. Serve slices directly from the pan with a generous dusting of confectioners' sugar. Keep the bars, wrapped, in the refrigerator for up to 3 days.

The Who, What, and Why of *Extremely* Special Whipped Cream

I know, I know: what's with the *Extremely* Special Whipped Cream (page 230), how did I discover it, and why am I so obsessed with it? Well, the short answer is this: I wanted to pitch a story to a popular online food site about my deep love of marshmallows, and while researching them, I learned that if you combine melted marshies with heavy cream, spectacularly delicious *stable* whipped cream is yours for the taking. And, although you may not care about whipped cream that has staying power, to me that notion is pure magic. When developing the recipes for my first book, *Icebox Cakes*, I was struck with how fab it would be if the whipped cream for the cakes was just a little more resilient. When you icebox cake (yes, it's a verb), your cake needs to rest in the fridge overnight. And although you may *have* whipped cream left over from cake assembly, you can't really chill it overnight

and then spread it over the cake in the morning, 'cause that's just not how whipped cream rolls. It gets watery after a few hours. But if you add melted marshies to it, we're talking game-changer, as the gelatin in the marshmallows sets the cream, not only providing it with longevity but with subtle marshie flavor, as well. I mean, if I can make the whipped cream *now* that is going to top the Easiest-Peasiest Chocolate Marshmallow Mousse, (page 106), or Individual Butterscotch Puddings (page 180), or Peppermint Stick No-Churn Ice Cream Sundaes (page 163), that I'm planning on serving after dinner tonight, or tomorrow, or next Tuesday, I am one happy peep. Enter the *Extremely* Special stuff—which is the stuff of which make-ahead dreams are made—as well as just a super-tasty, long-lasting accompaniment to so many delicious snackable bakes.

Better-Than-Apple-Pie Bars

MAKES 16 BARS
ACTIVE TIME: 20 MINUTES
BAKE TIME: 60 TO 65 MINUTES

Cooking spray or softened
unsalted butter for pan

FOR THE CRUMB TOPPING AND CRUST

2 cups (260 g) all-purpose flour,
plus more for flouring your
fingers

¾ cup (150 g) granulated sugar

¼ teaspoon kosher salt

10 tablespoons (142 g) unsalted
butter, cold and cubed

1 large egg

1 teaspoon vanilla extract

FOR THE APPLE FILLING

¼ cup plus 2 tablespoons (75 g)
granulated sugar

1½ tablespoons all-purpose flour

¾ teaspoon ground cinnamon

¼ teaspoon kosher salt

4 to 5 medium apples (about
1½ pounds; 684 g), peeled,
cored, and thinly sliced
(about ¼ inch thick)

1½ tablespoons freshly squeezed
lemon juice

Confectioners' sugar for dusting

Apple pie is great and all, but apple pie bars are, well, *better*. I like Honeycrisp and Pink Ladies in these bars, but I won't lie: Granny Smiths are my go-to. The crumb topping and crust can be made old-school style with your hands (which are the best tools in the kitchen, FYI), but if you use your food processor, you will def save time. But you do you: if lugging out a machine and then having to clean it and put it away again gives you agita (which, honestly, I am feeling just writing this), then stick to those hands: they will never steer you wrong. The crumb topping and crust soften a bit on day two, and that is hardly a bad thing.

1. Heat the oven to 375°F. Grease an 8-inch square cake pan with cooking spray or softened butter. Line the pan with a long piece of parchment paper that extends up and over two opposite sides of the pan.

2. To make the crumb topping and crust by hand, whisk together the flour, granulated sugar, and salt in a large bowl. Rub the butter into the dry ingredients using your fingers, until the butter is crumbly and pea-sized. Stir in the egg and vanilla with a fork, or your hands, until the mixture holds together when squeezed. Alternatively, to make the topping and crust with a food processor, pulse the dry ingredients and the butter in the bowl of the processer until the butter is pea-sized, then pulse in the egg and vanilla.

3. Remove 1½ cups (230 g) of the crumb mixture and refrigerate in a small bowl. Evenly press the remaining mixture into the bottom of the prepared pan with floured fingers, dock with a fork, and bake for about 15 minutes, or until you have finished preparing the filling.

4. To make the apple filling, whisk together the granulated sugar, flour, cinnamon, and salt in the same large bowl in which you made the crust and topping—no need to clean it first. Add the apples and toss to coat with a flexible spatula or your hands. Sprinkle with the lemon juice and toss a final time. Remove the crust from the oven, if you have not already, and carefully cover the warm bottom crust with the filling, pressing it down lightly. Sprinkle with the remaining chilled dough, using your fingers to pinch off and create crumbs, and gently press to adhere.

5. Lower the oven temperature to 350°F and bake for 60 to 65 minutes, rotating at the halfway point, until the crumb topping is lightly browned and the apples bubble around the edges and are soft in the center. Remove from the oven and let cool to room temperature. Serve straight from the pan or lift the bars out of the pan by the parchment overhang, running a butter knife around the edges. Dust with confectioners' sugar, slice, and serve. Keep the bars in an airtight container in the refrigerator for up to 3 days.

Favorite Any Berry Crisp

MAKES ABOUT 9 SERVINGS
ACTIVE TIME: 10 MINUTES
BAKE TIME: 65 TO 70 MINUTES

FOR THE TOPPING

1 cup (130 g) all-purpose flour

1 teaspoon baking powder

¼ teaspoon kosher salt

¾ cup (150 g) granulated sugar

½ cup (113 g) unsalted butter, cold and cubed

FOR THE FILLING

½ cup (100 g) granulated sugar

3 tablespoons cornstarch

¼ teaspoon kosher salt

6 cups (800 g) mixed berries, fresh or frozen

1 teaspoon vanilla extract

1 tablespoon freshly squeezed lemon juice

VARIATIONS

For Strawberry Brown Sugar Crisp, substitute 6 cups (900 g) halved strawberries for the mixed berries, and light brown sugar for the granulated in the topping. For Sweet (or Sour) Cherry Crisp, substitute 6 cups (800 g) pitted and chopped cherries for the berries, and 1 teaspoon almond extract for the vanilla. For Vanilla Stone Fruit Crisp, substitute 6 cups (930 g) of sliced plums or peaches for the berries, and increase the vanilla to 2 teaspoons.

So, I am very much pro-crisp, and am a little less enthusiastic about oaty crumbles—although I have included a uniquely delightful one in Chapter 7 (page 198), because I realize I am in the minority here. And this particular crisp includes not only my ideal ratio of butter to sugar to flour, but an unusual crisp ingredient as well: baking powder. I learned about the inclusion of BP in a crisp (it imparts a toothsome tenderness) from my buddies at the Kitchn and have never looked back. For the filling, I like strawberries, blackberries, and raspberries—but I've included a few variations if you're not feeling berry berry. Finally, this crisp takes a little over an hour to bake—and you will hate me for it, I get it, but a long bake time ensures a crispy and baked-through topping (and honestly, soggy toppings, are as bad as soggy bottoms, in my book).

1. Heat the oven to 400°F. Have ready an 8-inch square cake pan or a 2-quart baking dish, as well as a baking sheet.

2. To make the topping, whisk together the flour, baking powder, salt, and sugar in a medium bowl. Rub in the butter with your fingers, until the mixture holds together when squeezed. Refrigerate while you prepare the berries.

3. To make the filling, whisk together the sugar, cornstarch, and salt in a large bowl. Add the berries, vanilla, and lemon juice, toss with a flexible spatula to combine, and place in the pan. Sprinkle half of the topping over the fruit, breaking it and rolling it into different-sized pieces between your fingers. Refrigerate the remaining topping.

4. Place the pan on a baking sheet if it looks super full and bake for 25 minutes. Remove the pan from the oven, sprinkle on the rest of the topping, lower the heat to 375°F, and bake for an additional 38 to 43 minutes, until the crumb is lightly browned in the center. Remove from the oven and let cool briefly, 15 to 30 minutes, and serve.

5. Keep the crisp, wrapped, on the counter or in the refrigerator for up to 3 days.

Rhubarb Cobbler with Easy-Peasy Biscuits

MAKES ABOUT 9 SERVINGS
ACTIVE TIME: 10 MINUTES
BAKE TIME: 40 TO 45 MINUTES

FOR THE FILLING

¾ to 1 cup (150 to 200 g) granulated sugar

2 to 3 tablespoons cornstarch

¼ teaspoon kosher salt

6 cups (680 g) chopped rhubarb, fresh or frozen, cut into 1-inch pieces (about 1½ pounds; if stalks are super fat, slice them in half before cutting into pieces)

1½ teaspoons vanilla extract

FOR THE BISCUITS

1 cup (140 g) self-rising flour

3 tablespoons granulated sugar

¼ teaspoon kosher salt

1 cup (240 g) sour cream

1 teaspoon vanilla extract

FOR THE EGG WASH

1 large egg

¼ teaspoon kosher salt

Turbinado sugar for sprinkling

VARIATION

For Strawberry Rhubarb Cobbler with Easy-Peasy Biscuits, substitute 3 cups (420 g) of hulled and chopped strawberries for 3 cups (340 g) of the rhubarb.

This is inspired by an ancient but beloved *Bon Appétit* recipe for blueberry cobbler. I adore rhubarb, however, and so my version calls for that, along with biscuits made from self-rising flour, which snackable bakers, like myself, love for its ease of use, but if you don't have any on hand and don't want to invest in a bag, see page 14 for how to make your own. And I'm a tad "rangy" in this recipe, in that I offer a range of cornstarch, as some prefer their rhubarb on the extra juicy and loose side (2 tablespoons) and some prefer it more gelled (3 tablespoons), and a range of sugar, too, as some are not quite as sweet-toothed as yours truly and—bottom line—I aim to please. If you can find it, rhubarb with a deep pink hue makes for the prettiest of cobblers.

1. Heat the oven to 400°F. Have ready an 8-inch square cake pan or a 2-quart baking dish.

2. To make the filling, whisk together the granulated sugar, cornstarch, and salt in a large bowl. Add the rhubarb and vanilla and stir with a flexible spatula until all the rhubarb is coated. Transfer the rhubarb to the baking dish, evenly sprinkling any loose cornstarch mixture over the top.

3. To make the biscuits, whisk together the flour, granulated sugar, and salt in a large bowl. Stir in the sour cream and vanilla with a flexible spatula until the dough comes together in a single mass. Don't overmix. Portion the dough with a 2-tablespoon portion scoop or with measuring spoons and drop each biscuit directly on top of the rhubarb, flattening gently with your hands. You will have about 12 of them.

4. To make the egg wash, combine the egg and salt in a small bowl, using a fork. Brush the egg wash on each biscuit and sprinkle with turbinado sugar. Bake for 40 to 45 minutes, until the biscuits are golden brown and the rhubarb bubbles. Remove from the oven and let cool briefly before serving. Keep the cobbler, wrapped, on the counter for up to 3 days.

Brown Sugar Fruit Slump

MAKES ABOUT 9 SERVINGS
ACTIVE TIME: 10 MINUTES
COOK TIME: 25 MINUTES

FOR THE DUMPLINGS

1½ cups (195 g) all-purpose flour

3 tablespoons light brown sugar

2½ teaspoons baking powder

½ teaspoon kosher salt

½ teaspoon freshly grated nutmeg, ground cinnamon, or ground ginger (optional)

¾ cup (177 ml) heavy cream, at room temperature

3 tablespoons unsalted butter, melted and cooled slightly

FOR THE FRUIT

4 cups (535 g) mixed berries or (620 g) chopped stone fruit, fresh or frozen

½ cup (100 g) light brown sugar

¼ teaspoon kosher salt

¼ cup (59 ml) water

I mean, what the what the: how come no one ever told me about fruit slump?! If you, too, are in the dark, allow me to show you the fruit-slump light: fruit slump is cooked fruit (just enough to soften and draw out the juices) topped with lightly spiced brown sugar dumplings. No, it is not the prettiest of summer desserts, but it is one of the easiest and most perfect, as making a slump does not require an oven—it's a stovetop sitch of the yummiest caliber. A drizzle of heavy cream over your slump is nothing short of mandatory, just sayin'.

1. To make the dumplings, whisk together the flour, brown sugar, baking powder, salt, and your choice of spice (if using) in a medium bowl. Pour in the cream and butter and stir to combine with a flexible spatula. Let the dumpling dough rest while you prepare the fruit.

2. To prepare the fruit, place it in a 10-inch skillet, sprinkle with the brown sugar, salt, and water, and cook over medium-high heat, stirring with a flexible spatula, until bubbling. Lower the heat to medium and let simmer until the juices have the consistency of syrup, 5 to 10 minutes, depending on the fruit.

3. Portion the dough into small dumplings—about 3 tablespoons each—using a portion scoop or a couple of measuring spoons, and evenly blanket the fruit with them.

4. Cover the skillet, and over medium to medium-high heat, let the fruit bubble and the dumplings cook for about 15 minutes. The dumplings are ready when a wooden skewer inserted into the center of one comes out clean and the tops are dry to the touch.

5. If you'd like, to give the cooked dumplings a little color as well as a lightly toasted flavor, turn on the broiler and place an oven rack about 6 inches from it. Transfer the skillet to the rack and broil for about 1 minute, watching closely, until the dumplings are lightly browned. Remove from the oven and let sit for about 5 minutes. Slump is best the day it is made, but will keep, wrapped, on the counter for up to 3 days.

Raspberry Crumb-Topped Pie with Easiest Ever Crust and Crumble

MAKES ONE 9-INCH PIE
ACTIVE TIME: 20 MINUTES
BAKE TIME: 65 TO 70 MINUTES

FOR THE TOPPING

1 cup (130 g) all-purpose flour
½ cup (100 g) granulated sugar
½ cup (113 g) unsalted butter, melted and cooled slightly

FOR THE CRUST

2 cups (260 g) all-purpose flour
¾ teaspoon kosher salt
1 tablespoon granulated sugar
½ teaspoon baking powder
½ cup (113 g) unsalted butter, melted and cooled slightly
¼ cup (59 ml) whole milk, plus more for brushing

FOR THE RASPBERRIES

1 cup (200 g) granulated sugar
¼ cup (28 g) cornstarch
½ teaspoon kosher salt
5 cups (625 g) raspberries, fresh or frozen
1 tablespoon freshly squeezed lemon juice

Before you tell me pies aren't "snackable," let me just say this entire shebang is assembled in 20 MINUTES! It's snack time, my friends, that's all I can say. The crumble is of the stir-together-and-freeze variety. The crust calls for melted butter and is a press-in-the-pan sitch. And the berries are berries: you toss them with lemon juice, sugar, and cornstarch and you're done. Raspberry pie is kind of my number one, and if it is crumb topped, all the better, 'cause crumb topped for life. The pie will take longer to bake than you'd like, but the extra time ensures your berries will be actively bubbling in the center and you'll have some nice color on the edges of your crust.

1. Heat the oven to 400°F and place a baking sheet on the middle shelf. Have ready a 9-inch pie plate.

2. To make the topping, stir together all the topping ingredients in a small bowl, using a fork, until the mixture holds together when squeezed, and place in the freezer.

3. To make the crust, whisk together the flour, salt, sugar, and baking powder in a large bowl. Stir in the butter and milk with a fork until the mixture holds together when squeezed. Knead the dough a few times in the bowl with your hands and evenly press the dough onto the bottom and up the sides of the pie plate. Crimp the edges, brush them with milk, and place in the freezer.

4. To prepare the berries, whisk together the sugar, cornstarch, and salt in the same bowl in which you prepared the crust. No need to clean it. Stir in the berries and lemon juice with a flexible spatula. Transfer the berries to the crust and top with the crumble, pinching it into small, round(ish) crumbs. Place the pie on the preheated baking sheet and bake for 65 to 70 minutes, until the edges of the crust are golden brown and the berries are bubbling between the crumbs in the center of the pie. If the edges of the crust or the crumb takes on too much color while the pie bakes, cover with aluminum foil.

5. Remove from the oven and bring to room temperature before serving, about 4 hours. Keep the pie, wrapped, on the counter for up to 3 days.

Matt's Blueberry Galette with Easiest Ever Crust

MAKES ABOUT 8 SLICES
ACTIVE TIME: 15 MINUTES
BAKE TIME: 45 TO 50 MINUTES

FOR THE BLUEBERRIES
⅓ cup (67 g) granulated sugar

1 tablespoon cornstarch

¼ teaspoon kosher salt

2½ cups (365 g) blueberries, fresh or frozen

2 teaspoons vanilla extract

2 teaspoons freshly squeezed lemon juice

FOR THE CRUST
2 cups (260 g) all-purpose flour

¾ teaspoon kosher salt

1 tablespoon granulated sugar

½ teaspoon baking powder

½ cup (113 g) unsalted butter, melted and cooled slightly

¼ cup (59 ml) whole milk, cold, plus more for brushing

Turbinado sugar for sprinkling

My husband digs blueberries, I dig him, and we both dig this galette—but for different reasons. He loves it because it is exceptionally delicious and I love it because it is so darn easy to assemble. Get this: the Easiest Ever Crust here is made with *melted butter*! Yup, you heard that right: using it in a pie-crust, rather than very cold butter, means that there are no keeping-your-butter-cold issues and no resting and chilling and freezing, and (almost) no leaking! Yes, it will blow your mind, and, yes, you should stop reading this right now and go whip up this simple, non-fussy beauty for the blueberry lover in your life.

1. Heat the oven to 400°F. Have ready a baking sheet.

2. To prepare the blueberries, whisk together the granulated sugar, cornstarch, and salt in a medium bowl. Stir in the berries, vanilla, and lemon juice with a flexible spatula.

3. To make the crust, whisk together the flour, salt, granulated sugar, and baking powder in a large bowl. Stir in the butter and milk with a fork until the mixture holds together when squeezed. Knead the dough a few times in the bowl with your hands. Turn out the dough onto a long sheet of parchment paper and shape it into a flat disc in the center of the paper. Place another sheet of parchment paper on top and roll out the dough until it is about ¼ inch thick and round(ish) in shape. Place the dough, still between the sheets of paper, on the baking sheet and peel off the top sheet.

4. Transfer the berries to the center of the dough, leaving about a 2-inch border. Gently fold up the edges, decoratively squeezing the dough folds together. Brush them with milk and generously sprinkle with turbinado sugar.

5. Bake the galette for 45 to 50 minutes, rotating at the halfway point, until the filling is bubbling and the edges of the crust are lightly browned.

6. Remove from the oven and let cool briefly before slicing it with a pizza cutter, if you have one, or a sharp knife. Keep the galette, wrapped, on the counter or in the refrigerator for up to 3 days.

Orange Buttermilk Olive Oil Morning Muffins

MAKES 16 MUFFINS
ACTIVE TIME: 10 MINUTES
BAKE TIME: 20 MINUTES

1½ tablespoons orange zest
1¼ cups (250 g) granulated sugar
¾ cup (177 ml) extra-virgin olive oil
½ teaspoon vanilla extract
2 large eggs
¾ cup (177 ml) buttermilk
¼ cup plus 2 tablespoons (90 ml) freshly squeezed orange juice
½ teaspoon baking powder
¼ teaspoon baking soda
1 teaspoon kosher salt
1½ cups (195 g) all-purpose flour

There is a fab restaurant in NYC called Maialino and it is famous for—among other things—its olive oil cake. But despite its fame, I had never tasted the cake before the lovely former pastry chef at King (another super-special NYC restaurant) shared her version with me and I was smitten. The cake was so moist (I know, not everyone's favorite word—but it was) from the olive oil, with the most tender crumb and wonderful, yet subtle, citrus vibe. I was so taken with her cake, in fact, that a buttermilk breakfast muffin situation was born and here it is. I call these "morning muffins," but I honestly cannot imagine a time of day when they wouldn't be just perfect (and if you call them "cupcakes" and serve them as dessert with dollops of *Extremely* Special Whipped Cream [page 230], I promise not to tell a soul, as long as you invite me over).

1. Heat the oven to 350°F. Line a 12-well muffin tin with paper liners.

2. Rub the zest into the sugar with your fingertips in a large bowl. Whisk in the olive oil and vanilla for 30 seconds. Whisk in the eggs, one at a time, and then the buttermilk, followed by the orange juice. Sprinkle the baking powder, baking soda, and salt into the bowl, one at a time, vigorously whisking after each. Gently fold in the flour with a flexible spatula, just until the last streak disappears. The batter will be a little lumpy and thin.

3. Pour ¼ cup of batter into each prepared well and bake for about 20 minutes, or until the tops look dry and set and a wooden skewer inserted into the center of a muffin comes out with a moist crumb or two. Remove from the oven and let cool for about 5 minutes, or until you can safely remove the muffins from the tin without burning yourself. Repeat with the remaining batter.

4. Serve warm or at room temperature. Keep the muffins in an airtight container on the counter for up to 3 days.

Recipes and Inspo from My MIL

Unbeknownst to her, my mother-in-law is a snackable baker from way back. Her recipes check all the snackable boxes—easy, short ingredient lists, simple instructions, speedy assembly—and I reference them throughout the chapters in this book because I truly can't help myself, specifically her Buckle (page 66), her Oh Henry!® bars (page 127), and her Carrot Cake (page 221). I mean, not only is she an excellent baker (and cook), but it's *all* comfort food, *all* the time, and for me that just seals the deal. From mac-n-cheese made from a block of Velveeta and a jar of Cheez Whiz (please don't knock it till you've tried it) to leg of lamb with mint jelly (on Easter) to the best lobster rolls *ever* (we're talking Pepperidge Farm rolls grilled in butter alongside a small bag of Cape Cod potato chips, and we're talking heaven) to spectacular hot dogs (I know, hot dogs?! But yes: hot dogs), to pies and cakes and crisps and bar cookies, she can make anything and everything deliciously. And although she very occasionally plays a little hard to get when asked to share one of her unfussy recipes, with a little persistence she gives up the gold (in the form of a handwritten index card) and (usually) doesn't feign ignorance when you ask her to clarify a missing amount or illegible ingredient. Her recipe collection is vast, including those passed on to her by old friends and my husband's grandmother, as well as those she clipped from the back of a can or a box. But in addition, many come from my MIL's impressive magazine collection. From *Martha Stewart* to *Cook's Illustrated* to *Fine Cooking* to *Yankee Magazine* to many others I cannot even recall, for years, my mother-in-law read them all, transcribing the recipes that excited her and then saving the magazines themselves for a rainy day (aka me). In short, my MIL has not only inspired my snackable baking in the most traditional of ways—by sharing her recipes with me—but she also provided me with such an excellent "primary source," as it were, in the hundreds of magazines she sent me over the years. Even today, I love leafing through the recipes I saved from those old food mags. There's nothing like seeing Martha in some early '90s garb with a tray of cookies in hand, to really get the baking juices flowing.

Pear Sour Cream Snacking Cake

MAKES ONE 8-INCH SQUARE
CAKE

ACTIVE TIME: 10 MINUTES

BAKING TIME: 45 TO 50 MINUTES

Cooking spray or softened
  unsalted butter for pan

⅔ cup (158 ml) vegetable oil

1 cup (200 g) granulated sugar

2 teaspoons vanilla extract

2 large eggs

⅓ cup (80 g) sour cream

1½ teaspoons baking powder

¾ teaspoon ground cinnamon

¾ teaspoon kosher salt

1½ cups (195 g) all-purpose flour

2 medium pears, or apples
  (about 1 pound; 450 g), peeled,
  cored, and cut into ½-inch
  chunks

Turbinado sugar for sprinkling

In the early days of my marriage (not the Ice Age, but a while ago), my mother-in-law served me a slice of apple cake and to say I was awed that something without frosting or chocolate—or really any of the ingredients or components that typically excited me in a cake—could be so good, is an understatement. It was so simple and unassuming: just a sheet cake studded with chunks of apple, but I adored it and could not ask her fast enough for the recipe. Luckily, she neither judged me for the several pieces I'd consumed, nor wasted any time in transcribing the recipe onto a large index card in her easy-to-read, loopy cursive. It would be the first of many gloriously easy yet superb recipes that she would generously share with me over the years. Here, I've given the cake a "pear" makeover, and have no doubt that it will surprise you with its understated tastiness, as "Nonnie's" did me, just over a thousand years ago.

1. Heat the oven to 350°F. Grease an 8-inch square cake pan with cooking spray or softened butter. Line with a long piece of parchment paper that extends up and over two opposite sides of the pan.

2. Whisk together the oil, granulated sugar, and vanilla in a large bowl for 30 seconds. Whisk in the eggs and then the sour cream. Sprinkle the baking powder, cinnamon, and salt into the bowl, one at a time, vigorously whisking after each. Gently fold in the flour with a flexible spatula just until the last streak disappears. Scrape half the batter into the prepared pan, scattering half the pears on top, and repeat with the remaining batter and pears. Sprinkle with turbinado sugar and bake for 45 to 50 minutes, rotating the pan at the halfway point. The cake is done when a wooden skewer inserted into the center comes out with a moist crumb or two.

3. Remove from the oven and let cool in the pan about 20 minutes or until you can safely lift the cake out by the parchment overhang, without burning yourself. Run a butter knife around the edges if it resists. Let cool to room temperature before slicing and serving. Keep the cake, wrapped, on the counter for up to 3 days.

Banana Snacking Cake with Chocolate Malted Cream Cheese Frosting

MAKES ONE 8-INCH SQUARE CAKE
ACTIVE TIME: 20 MINUTES
BAKE TIME: 25 TO 30 MINUTES

Cooking spray or softened unsalted butter for pan

FOR THE CAKE
½ cup (113 g) unsalted butter, melted and cooled slightly
⅔ cup (133 g) light brown sugar
2 teaspoons vanilla extract
2 large eggs
¼ cup (59 ml) buttermilk
1 cup (230 g) mashed bananas (about 2 very ripe ones)
1 teaspoon baking soda
½ teaspoon kosher salt
1½ cups (195 g) all-purpose flour

FOR THE FROSTING
¼ cup (56 g) unsalted butter, at room temperature
4 ounces (113 g) cream cheese, at room temperature
1½ teaspoons vanilla extract
¼ teaspoon kosher salt
1¼ cups (150 g) confectioners' sugar
¼ cup (20 g) Dutch-processed cocoa powder
¼ cup (28 g) malted milk powder

Crushed malted milk balls for decorating

I kind of feel like the title of this recipe says it all. I mean just stringing together words like banana + snacking + chocolate + malt + cream cheese feels like enough. The cake is just so utterly flavorful (due to the combo of the buttermilk, brown sugar, and bananas) and the frosting is just about the softest and most luscious in the (snacking cake) land. I love chocolate and malt; and when you put a little cream cheese in the mix, need I say more? Make this now and thank me later.

1. Heat the oven to 350°F. Grease an 8-inch square cake pan with cooking spray or softened butter. Line with a long piece of parchment paper that extends up and over two opposite sides of the pan.

2. To make the cake, whisk together the butter, brown sugar, and vanilla in a large bowl for 30 seconds. Whisk in the eggs, followed by the buttermilk, and then the mashed bananas. Sprinkle the baking soda and salt into the bowl, one at a time, vigorously whisking after each. Gently fold in the flour with a flexible spatula just until the last streak disappears. Don't overmix.

3. Scrape the batter into the prepared pan and bake for 25 to 30 minutes, rotating the pan at the halfway point, until a wooden skewer inserted into the center comes out with only a moist crumb or two. Remove from the oven and let cool in the pan for about 20 minutes, or until you can safely lift the cake out by the parchment overhang without burning yourself. Run a butter knife around the edges if it resists. Let cool to room temperature before frosting.

4. To make the frosting, beat the butter and cream cheese on medium-low speed, in the bowl of a stand mixer fitted with the paddle attachment. Beat in the vanilla and salt, and then gradually the confectioners' sugar. Beat in the cocoa powder, followed by the malt powder, and beat to combine for an additional 30 seconds on medium speed. Generously frost the top of the cake, leaving the sides bare, or not, and sprinkle with the crushed candy. Cut into slices and serve. Keep the cake, wrapped, in the refrigerator for up to 3 days.

Black Forest Wacky(ish) Cake with Cherry Cream Cheese Whipped Cream

MAKES ONE 8-INCH SQUARE CAKE
ACTIVE TIME: 20 MINUTES
BAKE TIME: 25 TO 30 MINUTES

Cooking spray or softened
  unsalted butter for pan

FOR THE CAKE
1½ cups (195 g) all-purpose flour
⅓ cup (27 g) Dutch-processed
  cocoa powder
1 cup (200 g) light brown sugar
1 teaspoon baking soda
1 teaspoon kosher salt
1 cup (237 ml) whole milk
¼ cup plus 2 tablespoons (89 ml)
  vegetable oil
2 teaspoons vanilla extract
1 tablespoon white vinegar
½ cup (140 g) thick sweet or sour
  cherry preserves/jam

**FOR THE CHERRY CREAM
CHEESE WHIPPED CREAM**
4 ounces (113 g) cream cheese,
  at room temperature
1 cup (237 ml) heavy cream
1 tablespoon kirsch or other
  cherry-flavored alcohol, or to
  taste (optional)
1 teaspoon vanilla extract
⅓ cup (40 g) confectioners' sugar
1½ tablespoons cherry preserves/
  jam

Cherries for serving, if in season
  (optional)

This cake is wacky(ish) in a couple of ways: First, it is merely a riff on a traditional wacky cake, not an actual one (which is a vegan cake that replaces eggs and dairy with vinegar and water) and, second, I personally find it wacky, in the most wonderful of ways, because it has converted me from a hater of fruit and chocolate, to an extremely enthusiastic *lover*(!)—a feat of which I did not think any dessert was capable. But it happened: the cherry preserves and cherry-flavored whipped cream just marry so beautifully with the fudgy chocolate cake that I've jumped right on the fruit/chocolate bandwagon, and don't expect to be getting off any time soon. If you can (easily) find them, sour cherry preserves are wonderful here, and if you don't dig cherries, replace them with any jam that floats your fruity/chocolate boat—but choose a thick one, as opposed to a runnier one, as it will be easier to top the jam layer with the whipped cream if the jam has a tad more structure.

1. Heat the oven to 350°F. Grease an 8-inch square cake pan with cooking spray or softened butter. Line with a long piece of parchment paper that extends up and over two opposite sides of the pan.

2. To make the cake, whisk together the flour, cocoa powder, brown sugar, baking soda, and salt in a large bowl. Whisk together the milk, oil, vanilla, and vinegar in a 2-cup glass measuring cup. Pour the mixture over the dry ingredients and whisk until fully incorporated and smooth.

3. Scrape the batter into the prepared pan with a flexible spatula and bake for 25 to 30 minutes, until a wooden skewer inserted into the center of the cake comes out with a moist crumb or two. Remove from the oven and let cool in the pan for about 20 minutes, or until you can safely lift the cake out by the parchment overhang without burning yourself. Run a butter knife around the edges if it resists. Let cool to room temperature before spreading with the preserves and placing in the freezer for 10 minutes while you make the whipped cream. The time in the freezer will make it easier to spread the whipped cream without disturbing the layer of jam.

4. To make the whipped cream, whisk the cream cheese on medium speed in the bowl of a stand mixer fitted with the whisk attachment, just until smooth. Whisk in the cream, kirsch (if using), vanilla, and confectioners' sugar and continue to whisk on medium to medium-high speed until medium peaks form. Remove the bowl and fold in the jam by hand with a flexible spatula. Spread the cream over the cake, swirling it decoratively with an offset spatula or the back of a spoon, if you are feeling fancy; slice and serve with a few cherries (if using). Keep the cake, wrapped in plastic wrap, in the refrigerator for up to 3 days.

Strawberry Sheet Cake

ONE 9-BY-13-INCH
RECTANGULAR CAKE
ACTIVE TIME: 10 MINUTES
BAKE TIME: 55 TO 60 MINUTES

Cooking spray or softened
 unsalted butter for pan
1¼ cups (296 ml) vegetable oil
2¼ cups (450 g) granulated sugar
4 teaspoons vanilla extract
3 large eggs
1⅓ cups (315 ml) whole milk
1 tablespoon baking powder
1¼ teaspoons kosher salt
3 cups (390 g) all-purpose flour
1 pound (454 g) whole strawberries, fresh or frozen, hulled
 and roughly chopped
Turbinado sugar for sprinkling

So, you may not know it, but the summer of 2019 was the summer of strawberry sheet cakes. Both *Bon Appétit* and Deb Perelman (aka Smitten Kitchen) shared recipes for them; and I, too, had the berry sheet cake bug that summer, but developed a raspberry one, instead. But now that a little time has passed, I, too, am jumping on the strawberry bandwagon, because even just *saying* "strawberry sheet cake" gives me all the happy, summery feels. Can't exactly explain why, but it's true. This cake is easy. This cake is—well—*marvelous*. And this cake needs baking ASAP.

1. Heat the oven to 350°F. Grease a 9-by-13-inch pan with cooking spray or softened butter. Line with a long piece of parchment paper that extends up and over the two long sides of the pan.

2. Whisk together the oil, granulated sugar, and vanilla in a large bowl for 30 seconds. Whisk in the eggs, one at a time, and then the milk. Sprinkle the baking powder and salt into the bowl, one at a time, vigorously whisking after each. Gently fold in the flour with a flexible spatula just until the last streak disappears. The batter will be lumpy.

3. Scrape the batter into the prepared pan and evenly scatter the strawberries on top.

4. Generously sprinkle the cake with the turbinado sugar and bake for 55 to 60 minutes, rotating the cake at the halfway point. The cake is done when a wooden skewer inserted into the center comes out with a moist crumb or two.

5. Remove from the oven and let cool to room temperature. Serve slices directly from the pan; or lift the cake from the pan with the parchment overhang, running a butter knife around the edges if it resists. Keep the cake, wrapped, on the counter for up to 3 days.

Purplicious Summer Pudding for the Win

MAKES ABOUT 8 SERVINGS
ACTIVE TIME: 15 MINUTES
INACTIVE TIME: 6 HOURS
OR OVERNIGHT

6 cups (800 g) mixed berries,
    fresh or frozen
⅔ cup (133 g) granulated sugar
¼ teaspoon kosher salt
¼ cup (59 ml) water
1 to 2 tablespoons freshly
    squeezed lemon juice
1 pound (454 g) sliced white
    bread, crusts removed and
    cut in half

Now, bear with me here, but if slightly sweetened berries could be miraculously smooshed and molded together into the form of a cake, then they would be a summer pudding. I mean, although said pudding (which is a pudding in the British sense of the word, meaning "dessert," not in the American) *technically* includes bread, you can't taste it once the soft bread is drenched in berry-liciousness. In short, we're talking very fruity, very summery, and very—you guessed it: easy. Served with a drizzle of heavy cream, it makes for either the most charming and special of mid-July dinner-party-on-the-patio desserts or the most lovely of no-need-to-feel-guilty-about-eating-pudding-first-thing-in-the-morning breakfasts.

1. Line a 1½-quart bowl with two long pieces of plastic wrap that extend over and cover the sides of the bowl.

2. Combine the berries, sugar, salt, and water in a large pot over medium heat and cook until the berries release their juices and bubble, 5 to 8 minutes. Off the heat, add the lemon juice, stir, and strain the berries, reserving the juice in a medium shallow bowl.

3. Dip the halved slices of bread in the reserved juice, one at a time, and line the entire interior of the prepared bowl with the soaked bread, overlapping where necessary. Place half of the berries in the bowl and cover with additional pieces of soaked bread. Repeat with the other half of the berries and the remaining bread, pressing down lightly with your hands. Use the plastic wrap overhang to cover the pudding and place a plate on top that nestles just inside the bowl, resting directly on the pudding. Weigh down the pudding by placing a can of beans or a jar of spaghetti sauce on top of the plate. Refrigerate for at least 6 hours, up to overnight.

4. Remove the weight and plate and peel back the plastic wrap. Invert the pudding onto a serving plate, remove the bowl and plastic wrap, cut the pudding into slices as you would a cake, and serve. Keep the pudding, wrapped, in the refrigerator for up to 3 days.

Luscious Lemon Possets

MAKES ABOUT 6 PUDDINGS
ACTIVE TIME: 20 MINUTES
INACTIVE TIME: 3 HOURS

2 cups (474 ml) heavy cream

¾ cup (150 g) granulated sugar

2 tablespoons lemon zest

¼ teaspoon kosher salt

½ cup (118 ml) freshly squeezed
    lemon juice

A posset is a softly set stovetop pudding with a texture as ethereal as a baked custard—in other words, the kind of texture a cornstarch-thickened pudding can only dream about. Possets are just magic in my book and with the most whimsical of names, to boot. The ½ cup of lemon juice makes for an ultra-lemony posset, but it also makes for a softly set one. For a slightly firmer texture and a slightly less lemony vibe, reduce the lemon juice by 1 to 3 tablespoons.

1. Have ready six 6-ounce ramekins.

2. Combine the cream, sugar, zest, and salt in a medium saucepan and bring to a boil over medium-high heat, stirring occasionally with a flexible spatula. Let boil for 5 minutes, without stirring, watching closely so that the mixture does not boil over. Off the heat, add the lemon juice and let sit for 15 to 20 minutes to cool. Whisk briefly and pour through a fine wire mesh sieve to remove the zest.

3. Divide the posset evenly among the six ramekins and refrigerate until set, at least 3 hours. Serve straight-up for a pucker-punch, or with a handful of berries for a veritable party in your mouth. Keep the possets, wrapped, in the refrigerator for up to 3 days.

CHAPTER 2.

(Never Plain) Vanilla

This chapter is for all the vanilla lovers in the house—a less vocal sweets-loving faction than those on team chocolate, but equally as important. I, myself, am *very* vanilla forward, despite being an equal opportunity treats-lover. In fact, my recipes tend to call for a *glug* of vanilla extract, as opposed to a mere teaspoon. But you do you. If you want to pull back on the vanilla in your crumb cake or buckle or crispy rice cereal treats, I promise not to stand in your way. And remember, vanilla not only provides baked goods and sweets with its own lovely, slightly sweet, and caramelly flavor, but it is also an extremely enthusiastic team player, encouraging the other flavors in the mixture to really pop (such as the cinnamon in the snacking cake's crumb topping and the chocolate in the no-bake cheesecake crust) and we love it for that. Moreover, because vanilla *adores* fruit, and fruit feels similarly about vanilla, I have included a handful of fruity/vanilla combos herein, such as plum vanilla and cherry vanilla (I know: I think of *everything*). Finally, just in case you've got some notion that sweets featuring vanilla must be boring (compared to those featuring chocolate, for instance), I am certain the following treats will steer you on the path toward a state of deep and meaningful vanilla-appreciation, and one from which you may never look back.

Otherworldly Vanilla Cream Scones

MAKES 8 SCONES
ACTIVE TIME: 8 MINUTES
BAKE TIME: 20 TO 25 MINUTES

2 cups (260 g) all-purpose flour,
  plus more for dusting
½ cup (100 g) granulated sugar,
  plus more for sprinkling
1 tablespoon baking powder
1 teaspoon kosher salt
1 cup (237 ml) heavy cream,
  plus more for brushing
1 tablespoon vanilla extract

VARIATION

For Otherworldly Vanilla
Rhubarb Cream Scones, stir
1 cup (113 g) chopped rhubarb
(½-inch pieces) into the
dough along with the liquid
ingredients.

I mean, I don't know what to tell you: these are truly special scones, which leaves one particularly speechless in light of how breathtakingly easy they are to assemble. They are tender, flavorful, and rich and I might deserve some kind of MacArthur Genius Grant for having developed them. If you want slightly taller scones and are into delayed(ish) gratification, do not begin heating your oven until *after* you assemble the scones, and while it comes to temp, chill the scones in the freezer.

1. Heat the oven to 375°F and line a baking sheet with parchment paper.

2. Whisk together the flour, sugar, baking powder, and salt in a large bowl. Whisk together the cream and vanilla in a glass measuring cup. Pour the wet mixture over the flour mixture and stir with a flexible spatula until a shaggy dough forms.

3. Dump the dough onto a generously floured work surface. Flour your hands and gather it into a rectangle, with a long side nearest you. Fold the two short ends into the center of the rectangle, one at a time, overlapping them, as you would when folding a letter. Rotate the rectangle so a long side is again nearest you, roll out the rectangle with a rolling pin, and repeat the folds twice more, for a total of three complete letter folds. Roughly shape the dough into a 7-inch round and slice into eight wedges, as you would a pizza, with a bench scraper or chefs' knife. Place on the prepared baking sheet. Brush the scones with cream and sprinkle them with sugar.

4. Bake for 20 to 25 minutes, rotating at the halfway point, until the tops and bottoms of the scones are nicely browned. Remove from the oven and let the scones cool on the baking sheet for about 5 minutes before serving with loads of salted butter and jam. The scones are best the day they are made, but will keep in an airtight container on the counter for up to 3 days.

Extra Crumb Snacking Cake

MAKES ONE 8-INCH SQUARE CAKE
ACTIVE TIME: 15 MINUTES
BAKING TIME: 55 TO 60 MINUTES

Cooking spray or softened
   unsalted butter for pan

FOR THE CRUMB TOPPING
2¼ cups (277 g) cake flour
1 cup packed (200 g) dark brown
   sugar
1½ teaspoons ground cinnamon
¾ teaspoon kosher salt
¾ cup (169 g) unsalted butter,
   cold and cubed

FOR THE CAKE
½ cup vegetable oil
1 cup (200 g) granulated sugar
1½ teaspoons vanilla extract
2 large eggs
½ cup (115 g) sour cream
¼ teaspoon baking powder
¼ teaspoon baking soda
¾ teaspoon kosher salt
1½ cups (185 g) cake flour

My nostalgic love of packaged snack cakes is well-documented and although my softest spot might be for Hostess Twinkies and Drake's Devil Dogs, I've also a weakness for Drake's Coffee Cakes. Here, I pay special homage to them, but in snacking cake form. Now, I know purchasing a box of cake flour for this recipe is not on your list of fun things to do, but the softness of the crumb topping and tenderness of the cake owe everything to it, and you won't want to miss out on that. Moreover, you can make your own cake flour—see page 14 for the how-to.

1. Heat the oven to 350°F and grease an 8-inch square cake pan with cooking spray or softened butter. Line with a long sheet of parchment paper that extends up and over two opposite ends of the pan.

2. To make the crumb topping, whisk together the cake flour, brown sugar, cinnamon, and salt in a medium bowl. Rub in the butter with your fingers until small (and big) crumbs form. Refrigerate while you make the cake batter.

3. To make the cake, whisk together the oil, granulated sugar, and vanilla in a large bowl for 30 seconds. Whisk in the eggs, one at a time, and then the sour cream. Sprinkle the baking powder, baking soda, and salt into the bowl, one at a time, vigorously whisking after each. Sift the cake flour over the wet ingredients and gently fold it in with a flexible spatula just until the last streak disappears. The batter will be lumpy. Don't overmix.

4. Scrape the batter into the prepared pan and sprinkle with the chilled crumbs. Bake for 55 to 60 minutes, rotating the pan at the halfway point. The cake is done when a wooden skewer inserted into the center comes out with only a moist crumb or two and the crumbs are lightly browned.

5. Remove from the oven and let cool in the pan for about 20 minutes, or until you can safely lift the cake out by the parchment overhang without burning yourself. Run a butter knife around the edges if it resists. Serve warm or at room temperature. Keep the cake, wrapped, on the counter for up to 3 days.

Cranberry Vanilla Breakfast Buckle

MAKES ABOUT 9 SERVINGS
ACTIVE TIME: 15 MINUTES
BAKE TIME: 65 TO 70 MINUTES

Cooking spray or softened
   unsalted butter for pan

FOR THE TOPPING

1 cup packed (200 g) light brown
   sugar

1 cup (130 g) all-purpose flour

¼ teaspoon kosher salt

½ cup (113 g) unsalted butter, cold
   and cubed

1 teaspoon vanilla extract

FOR THE CAKE

¼ cup (56 g) unsalted butter,
   melted and cooled slightly

⅔ cup (133 g) light brown sugar

2 teaspoons vanilla extract

1 large egg

⅓ cup (79 ml) heavy cream or
   whole milk

1½ teaspoons baking powder

½ teaspoon kosher salt

2 cups (190 g) cranberries, fresh
   or frozen, roughly chopped

1½ cups (195 g) all-purpose flour

Confectioners' sugar for dusting

I was first introduced to the berry-filled world of buckles by my husband, as his mother's is a breakfast cake to end all breakfast cakes. Not having grown up in a home of buckles, I hadn't a clue as to what to expect when experiencing my MIL's for the first time; and, if you, too, have been buckle-less until now, no worries: I got you. A buckle is essentially a whimsical name for a fruit-filled coffeecake, but one in which the batter bakes up and over the fruit, giving it a "buck-led" appearance. I like mine, like my mother-in-law's, with a crumble topping, so that is what you will find here, along with loads of tart, juicy cranberries and a vanilla-infused, tender crumbed-cake. The batter is thickkkkk and so takes a looooong time to bake, but yes, it is worth it, and yes, you can substitute a different berry in your buckle (including blue-berries—and if you do, my husband will happily take a slice, as "bloobs," as we affectionately call them in my house, are his favorite).

1. Heat the oven to 350°F. Grease an 8-inch square cake pan with cooking spray or softened butter. Line with a long piece of parchment paper that extends up and over two opposite edges of the pan.

2. To make the topping, whisk together the brown sugar, flour, and salt in a medium bowl. Rub in the butter, using your fingers, drizzle in the vanilla, and continue to rub until the mixture holds together when squeezed. Refrigerate while you make the cake.

3. To make the cake, whisk together the butter, brown sugar, and vanilla in a large bowl for about 30 seconds. Whisk in the egg and then the heavy cream. Sprinkle the baking powder and salt into the bowl, one at a time, vigorously whisking after each. Gently fold 1½ cups (143 g) of the cranberries into the wet ingredients, along with the flour, with a flexible spatula, just until the last streak of flour disappears. Don't overmix. The batter will be very thick. Scrape the batter into the prepared pan and sprinkle the remaining cranberries on top. Pinching the chilled topping between your fingers to form crumbs, evenly cover the cake with it.

4. Bake for 65 to 70 minutes, rotating the pan at the halfway point, until a wooden skewer inserted into the center comes out with only a moist crumb or two.

5. Remove from the oven and let cool in the pan for about 20 minutes, or until you can safely lift the buckle out by the parchment overhang without burning yourself. Run a butter knife around the edges if it resists. Let cool to room temperature before dusting with confectioners' sugar, slicing into squares, and serving. Keep the buckle, wrapped, on the counter for up to 3 days.

Jumbo Vanilla Cherry Sour Cream Muffins

MAKES 6 JUMBO MUFFINS OR
12 STANDARD MUFFINS
ACTIVE TIME: 10 MINUTES
BAKE TIME: 35 TO 40 MINUTES

Cooking spray or softened
　　unsalted butter for pan
⅓ cup (79 ml) vegetable oil
1¼ cups (250 g) granulated sugar
2 tablespoons vanilla extract
2 large eggs
⅔ cup (150 g) full-fat sour cream
1½ teaspoons baking powder
¼ teaspoon baking soda
1 teaspoon kosher salt
2 cups (260 g) all-purpose flour
2 cups (280 g) coarsely chopped
　　cherries, fresh or frozen, plus
　　a handful for topping
Turbinado sugar for (generous)
　　sprinkling

Yes, there are 2 tablespoons of vanilla extract in these muffins, and yes that's a lot, but I'm a self-proclaimed vanilla addict, hence the large amount (and, cherry-vanilla is kind of a match made in heaven, so there's that, too). As for the size of these vanilla-bombs, well, jumbo is my jam, I cannot lie; and although I know bigger is not *always* better, when it comes to these fluffy, tender, vanilla-forward cherry muffins, bigger wins every time. If you don't have a jumbo muffin tin, or are anti-jumbo, don't fret: the recipe also makes 12 lovely, standard-sized muffins.

1. Heat the oven to 400°F and generously grease a 6-well jumbo muffin tin with cooking spray or softened butter. If using a standard muffin tin, you may use paper liners.

2. Whisk together the oil, granulated sugar and vanilla in a large bowl for 30 seconds. Whisk in the eggs, one at a time, and then the sour cream. Sprinkle the baking powder, baking soda, and salt into the bowl, one at a time, vigorously whisking after each.

3. Gently fold the flour and the cherries into the wet ingredients with a flexible spatula just until the last streak of flour disappears. Divide the batter among the prepared muffin wells and press a few chopped cherries onto the top of each before generously sprinkling with turbinado sugar.

4. Bake for 35 to 40 minutes. At the halfway point, lower the oven temp to 350°F and rotate the tin. If baking standard-sized muffins, bake for 20 to 25 minutes. The muffins are ready when a wooden skewer inserted into the center of one comes out with only a moist crumb or two.

5. Remove from the oven and let cool in the tin for about 15 minutes, or until you can safely remove the muffins by running a butter knife around each one without burning yourself. Serve warm. Keep the muffins in an airtight container on the counter for up to 3 days.

VARIATIONS

For Jumbo Raspberry Lemon Sour Cream Muffins, substitute
2 cups (250 g) of raspberries for the chopped cherries, and add
1 tablespoon of lemon zest and 2 to 3 tablespoons of freshly
squeezed lemon juice, or to taste, when you add the sour cream.
For Jumbo Cinnamon Cranberry Sour Cream Muffins, substitute
2 cups (190 g) of coarsely chopped cranberries for the chopped
cherries, and whisk in 1½ teaspoons of ground cinnamon along
with the baking powder, baking soda, and salt. For Jumbo Vanilla
Strawberry Sour Cream Muffins, substitute 2 cups (260 g) of
coarsely chopped strawberries for the chopped cherries.

A Love Letter to Marshies (aka Marshmallows)

Here's the thing about marshmallows: I unequivocally adore them—and this, despite the fact that I am not a small child. I mean I think they might be on my list of top ten favorite foods (along with fried chicken and spaghetti and meatballs). Curiously, my soft spot for marshies is not all that long-lived. I mean, it goes without saying that I've been eating s'mores and Rice Krispies Treats® (aka RKTs) for forever, but it's not as if I ate straight-up marshmallows by the handful as a little kid or even bought them in bulk in college for late-night snacking fests with my roommates. In fact, it was when I first developed my own (dare I say) perfect version of RKTs (page 73) a few years back, that the love was born. During the development phase, many bags of mini marshies were purchased. But because the recipe I settled on called for one bag to be melted with the butter, plus one cup to be folded in whole (for melty marshie pockets—annoying, I know, but worth it), not all of the minis ended up in the treats—many just made their way straight into my mouth. And if you have never sat in front of the television watching something fab and nibbling on tiny marshmallows by the one or two, I behoove you to give it a go. When I learned that marshmallows (which are made with gelatin, for those not in the know) could be used in chocolate mousse not only to set it, but to provide it with an ethereal texture as well, I was sold. See page 106 to see this marshie-in-mousse magic in action. Typically, recipes for mousse require gelatin to thicken and set it—and I've used whipped egg whites to do so, as well. But I am not a huge gelatin fan (a little too fussy for this easy-peasy gal, and a little scary, to boot); nor am I a lover of egg white whipping (due to my aversion to pulling out my stand mixer). Thus, marshies to the mousse-rescue, in a big way. Now, not sure you could substitute marshies for gelatin in other applications, but if you are feeling adventurous and give it a go, please be in touch, stat, to let me know how it all went down. And—good news: you know where you *absolutely* need to be incorporating marshies? Whipped cream. When I discovered melted marshies could stabilize whipped cream, as they do in my *Extremely Special Whipped Cream* (page 230), my life took a turn for the better, no joke (see page 31 for all the scoops on that). Long story short, peeps, my affection for marshmallows, though still in its infancy, will not be waning any time soon. The stuff is pure sugar-sorcery.

Secret Ingredient Crispy Rice Cereal Treats

MAKES 16 TREATS
ACTIVE TIME: 10 MINUTES
INACTIVE TIME: 1 HOUR

Cooking spray or softened unsalted butter for pan and for your hands

½ cup (113 g) unsalted butter

⅓ cup (105 g) sweetened condensed milk

1 tablespoon vanilla extract

1 teaspoon kosher salt

One 10-ounce bag (283 g) mini marshmallows, plus 1 cup (40 g; optional)

6 cups (170 g) crispy rice cereal, such as Rice Krispies

VARIATION

For Milk Chocolate–Topped Secret Ingredient Crispy Rice Cereal Treats, spread the milk chocolate topping (omitting the tahini) from the Tahini Milk Chocolate Bars (page 127) over the cereal mixture after you press it into the pan. Place in the refrigerator for about an hour to set before slicing and serving.

Rice Krispies Treats® and I go way back. I literally treasure everything about them (and have since I was in elementary school)—the texture (sticky *and* crunchy), the flavor (marshmallowy *and* buttery) and the time it takes to make them (umh, practically none). And who knew they could be improved upon? But with the addition of a little sweetened condensed milk—a tip I learned from my friend Libby Willis, of the now defunct MeMe's Diner (RIP)—plus the extra minute it takes to melt the butter till brown, I think new and improved RKTs are in the house. The result is a creamy, almost caramelized flavor, as well as a soft and extra-chewy texture. And if you're smart enough to indulge in the optional extra cup of mini marshies, you will have pockets of gooey, slightly melted marshmallows throughout your treats, resulting in nothing short of RKT Heaven (and an open bag of mini marshies from which to nibble, to boot).

1. Grease an 8-inch square cake pan with cooking spray or softened butter. Line with a long piece of parchment paper that extends up and over two opposite sides of the pan.

2. Melt the butter in a large pot over medium to medium-high heat until it browns, smells nutty, and begins sputtering, 3 to 5 minutes. Stir in the sweetened condensed milk, vanilla, and salt with a flexible spatula until combined, and then the 10 ounces (283 g) of marshmallows until melted.

3. Off the heat, stir in the cereal and remaining cup (40 g) of marshmallows (if using), until combined. Transfer to the prepared pan, spray your hands with cooking spray or rub a little butter on them, and flatten the mixture lightly and evenly.

4. Let the treats set up on the counter for at least an hour, then lift them out of the pan, using the parchment paper overhang, and slice. Keep the treats in an airtight container on the counter for up to 3 days.

Strawberry-n-Cream Bar Cookies

MAKES 16 BARS
ACTIVE TIME: 10 MINUTES
BAKE TIME: ABOUT 20 MINUTES

Cooking spray or softened
   unsalted butter for pan
½ cup (113 g) unsalted butter,
   melted and cooled slightly
1 cup (200 g) granulated sugar
1½ teaspoons vanilla extract
1 large egg
¾ teaspoon kosher salt
¼ teaspoon baking powder
1 cup (130 g) all-purpose flour
¾ cup (120 g) chopped white
   chocolate, or chips
¾ cup (25 g) freeze-dried strawberries, crushed in your fist
   into dusty little bits, about
   ¼ inch, or smaller

So, tart strawberries and sweet cream is a yummy-sounding combo, am I right? And when the strawberries are of the freeze-dried variety, and the "cream" is white chocolate, and a buttery, blondie-type bar cookie is the vehicle that brings them together, yes: something delectable is, indeed, happening. Here, I am going to go completely off brand and suggest that an actual bar of white chocolate, chopped, works better than chips, as the chopped chocolate gets a tad meltier when baked. But they both work and give you strawberry-and-cream vibes in the most heavenly of ways possible.

1. Heat the oven to 375°F. Grease an 8-inch square cake pan with cooking spray or softened butter. Line with a long piece of parchment paper that extends up and over two opposite sides of the pan.

2. Whisk together the melted butter, sugar, and vanilla in a large bowl for 30 seconds. Whisk in the egg. Sprinkle the salt and baking powder into the bowl, one at a time, vigorously whisking after each. Fold in the flour with a flexible spatula until just a few streaks remain and then fold in the white chocolate and strawberries until the last streak disappears.

3. Evenly spread the (thick) dough in the prepared pan with a flexible spatula and bake for about 20 minutes, rotating at the halfway point. The bars are ready when lightly browned in the middle and darker brown around the edges. Don't overbake.

4. Remove from the oven. Let cool to room temperature in the pan and then lift the bars out by the parchment overhang. Run a butter knife around the edges if they resist and slice into 16 squares. Keep the bars in an airtight container on the counter for up to 3 days.

Dreamy "Thicc" and Chewy Sugar Cookies

MAKES 24 COOKIES
ACTIVE TIME: 10 MINUTES
BAKE TIME: 10 TO 12 MINUTES

⅓ cup (65 g) vegetable shortening

½ cup (113 g) unsalted butter, melted and cooled slightly

1 cup (200 g) granulated sugar, plus ½ cup (100 g) for rolling the cookies in and for sprinkling postbake

⅓ cup (110 g) light corn syrup

1½ tablespoons vanilla extract

1 large egg, cold

1 teaspoon baking soda

1 teaspoon kosher salt

2¾ cups (358 g) all-purpose flour

VARIATION

For Rainbow Sprinkle Dreamy "Thicc" and Chewy Sugar Cookies, whisk ½ cup (70 g) of rainbow sprinkles into the wet ingredients along with the flour.

I am a thick and chewy sugar cookie peep, as opposed to a thin and crispy one; and on the off chance you are, too—yay: pretty sure you are going to be into these deeply vanilla-flavored cuties. And I know, I know: shortening *and* corn syrup in a single recipe? But before you get your knickers in a twist, there's a good reason for the inclusion of both— corn syrup contributes to the cookies' chewiness and shortening helps them keep their shape without a long rest in the fridge so . . . you're welcome. But if shortening makes you crazy, substitute vegetable oil and chill your cookie dough until quite firm and cold prebake, at least 2 hours.

1. Heat the oven to 350°F. Line two baking sheets with parchment paper.

2. Whisk the shortening into the warm melted butter in a large bowl until the shortening melts (if there are still a few little solid bits of shortening, don't worry). Whisk in 1 cup (200 g) of the sugar, the corn syrup, and the vanilla, and then the egg. Sprinkle the baking soda and salt into the bowl, one at a time, vigorously whisking after each. Gently fold in the flour with a flexible spatula just until the last streak disappears. Don't overmix.

3. Place the remaining ½ cup (100 g) of sugar in a small, shallow bowl. Using a 2-tablespoon portion scoop, or measuring spoons, portion out 12 cookies per prepared baking sheet. Roll each one into a ball in your hands and then roll in the sugar to coat. Bake for 10 to 12 minutes, rotating and swapping the placement of the sheets at the halfway point, until the cookies are puffy, look dry, and are just beginning to slightly brown around the edges.

4. Remove from the oven and gently press the cookies with a spatula to flatten them, then sprinkle each with additional sugar. Eat warm (it's what all the cool kids do) or at room temperature. Keep the cookies in an airtight container on the counter for up to 3 days.

Plum Vanilla Upside-Down Snacking Cake

MAKES ONE 9-INCH ROUND CAKE
ACTIVE TIME: 15 MINUTES
BAKE TIME: 40 TO 45 MINUTES

Cooking spray or softened
  unsalted butter for pan

FOR THE PLUMS

¼ cup (56 g) unsalted butter,
  at room temperature

½ cup (100 g) granulated sugar

¼ teaspoon kosher salt

5 medium plums (about 1 pound;
  454 g), ripe, but not too ripe,
  unpeeled and cut into scant
  ½-inch wedges

FOR THE CAKE

½ cup (113 g) unsalted butter,
  melted and cooled slightly

1 cup (200 g) granulated sugar

1 tablespoon vanilla extract

2 large eggs

½ cup (118 ml) buttermilk

1½ teaspoons baking powder

¼ teaspoon baking soda

¾ teaspoon kosher salt

1½ cups (195 g) all-purpose flour

I love an upside-down cake and this plum vanilla one happens to be stunning to look at (and yes: looks *are* everything—joke) and beyond easy, as rather than cook the caramel "topping" on the stovetop before assembling the cake, you merely spread softened butter on the bottom of the pan, sprinkle with sugar, and once baked: voilà, caramel! To soften the butter quickly, place a stick, still in its paper, in the microwave, and microwave in 10-second bursts, rotating the stick by a quarter turn each time, for about four turns total.

1. Heat the oven to 350°F. Grease just the sides of a 9-inch cake pan with cooking spray or softened butter.

2. To prepare the plums, spread the butter over the bottom of the pan, using an offset spatula or the back of a spoon. Sprinkle the butter with the sugar and salt. Decoratively place the plums over the sugar, starting around the outer edges and working your way into the center, until the bottom of the pan is covered in plums.

3. To make the cake, whisk together the melted butter, sugar, and vanilla in a large bowl for 30 seconds. Whisk in the eggs, one at a time, and then the buttermilk. Sprinkle the baking powder, baking soda, and salt into the bowl, one at a time, whisking vigorously after each. Gently fold in the flour with a flexible spatula just until the last streak disappears. The batter will be lumpy. Don't overmix. Scrape the batter into the pan and evenly spread it over the plums.

4. Bake for 40 to 45 minutes, rotating at the halfway point, until a wooden skewer inserted into the center comes out with only a moist crumb or two. Remove from the oven and immediately run a paring knife around the edge of the pan. Let sit for 5 minutes and then carefully invert the cake onto a serving platter. If bits of plum stick to the bottom of the pan, carefully remove them and nudge them back onto the cake.

5. Let cool until the topping sets a bit, about 30 minutes, or to room temperature, then slice and serve. The cake is best the day it is made but will keep, wrapped, on the counter for up to 3 days.

Easiest Ever (No, Really) Rainbow Sprinkle Snacking Cake with Cream Cheese Glaze

MAKES ONE 8-INCH ROUND CAKE
ACTIVE TIME: 15 MINUTES
BAKE TIME: 45 MINUTES

Cooking spray or softened
    unsalted butter for pan

FOR THE CAKE
1½ cups (195 g) all-purpose flour
1 cup (200 g) granulated sugar
3 tablespoons rainbow sprinkles,
    plus more for decorating
1 teaspoon baking soda
¾ teaspoon kosher salt
1 cup (237 ml) cold tap water
5 tablespoons (75 ml) vegeta-
    ble oil
1 tablespoon vanilla extract
1 tablespoon white vinegar

FOR THE GLAZE
3 ounces (85 g) cream cheese,
    at room temperature
½ cup (60 g) confectioners' sugar
⅛ teaspoon kosher salt
2 tablespoons whole milk
½ teaspoon vanilla extract

Hello, (unintentionally) vegan cake, requiring not a single egg or drop of dairy. Sometimes called a "wacky" cake (What? No eggs or dairy? That's straight-up wacky!) or a "Depression" cake (as it ostensibly originated during the Great Depression when such items were pricey and scarce), I just call it outstanding (and with the addition of sprinkles, I also call it a darn good time). The cake could not be easier to assemble and the (non-vegan) cream cheese glaze is like a soft frosting. For a vegan version of this cake with a chocolate glaze, see the variations after the recipe.

1. Heat the oven to 350°F. Grease an 8-inch round cake pan with cooking spray or softened butter. Line the bottom with parchment paper.

2. To make the cake, whisk together the flour, granulated sugar, sprinkles, baking soda, and salt in a large bowl. Whisk in the water, oil, vanilla, and vinegar until fully incorporated and smooth. The batter will be thin. Pour it into the prepared pan and bake for 45 minutes, rotating at the halfway point. The cake is ready when a wooden skewer inserted into the center comes out with only a moist crumb or two.

3. Remove from the oven and let cool for 10 to 15 minutes, then invert the cake onto a cooling rack, right side up, running a knife around the edges if it resists. Let cool to room temperature before glazing.

4. To make the glaze, gently whisk (so as not to send sugar flying around your kitchen) together the cream cheese, confectioners' sugar, and salt in a medium bowl until combined and then vigorously whisk until smooth. Whisk in the milk and vanilla and spread decoratively over just the top of the cooled cake, leaving the outer edge and sides of the cake naked. Decorate with additional rainbow sprinkles. Refrigerate about 15 minutes to set the glaze before serving. Keep the cake, wrapped, in the refrigerator for up to 3 days.

VARIATIONS

For an Easiest Ever (No, Really) Chocolate Snacking Cake with Cream Cheese Glaze, omit the sprinkles, substitute light brown sugar for the granulated, whisk in ⅓ cup (27 g) Dutch-processed cocoa powder along with the flour, and add an additional tablespoon of vegetable oil. And for a full-on Vegan Easiest Ever (No, Really) Rainbow Sprinkle Snacking Cake with Chocolate Almond Glaze, replace the cream cheese glaze with the Chocolate Almond Glaze (page 139).

Vanilla No-Bake Cheesecake with a Chocolate Cookie Crust

ONE 9-INCH ROUND CAKE
ACTIVE TIME: 15 MINUTES
INACTIVE TIME: 5 HOURS TO
OVERNIGHT

Cooking spray or softened
  unsalted butter for pan

CRUST

9 ounces (255 g) crispy chocolate
  cookies

3 tablespoons granulated sugar

½ teaspoon kosher salt

7 tablespoons (99 g) unsalted butter, melted and cooled slightly

½ teaspoon vanilla extract

FILLING

16 ounces (453 g) cream cheese,
  at room temperature

One 14-ounce can (397 g) sweetened condensed milk

½ teaspoon kosher salt

3 tablespoons freshly squeezed
  lemon juice

2 teaspoons vanilla extract

Dutch-processed cocoa powder
  for dusting (optional)

VARIATION

For Lemon No-Bake Cheesecake
with a Graham Cracker Crust,
increase the lemon juice to
⅓ cup (79 ml); reduce the vanilla
to 1 teaspoon; replace the
cookies with 14 full-size graham
crackers (220 g; 2½ cups ground);
and omit the cocoa powder.

If you are new to the world of no-bake cheesecakes, welcome. They could not be easier to assemble (throw a few
things in a stand mixer and don't overmix) and because there
is no baking, just refrigerating, there are no scary cracked or
overbaked cheesecake situations with which to reckon. The
lemon juice helps the filling set but does not make the cake
lemony—however, if lemon is your jam, check out the variation.
Finally, this cheesecake, though perfect, does not have the tall-
est of statures and thus will answer to "cheesecake torte" or
"cheesecake tart," in case you were wondering.

1. Grease a 9-inch springform pan with cooking spray or softened
   butter. Line the bottom and sides with parchment paper.

2. To make the crust, process the cookies, sugar, and salt in the bowl
   of a food processor until the cookies are finely ground. Pour in the
   butter and vanilla and process until the mixture holds together
   when squeezed. Alternatively, you may place the dry ingredients
   in a sealed resealable plastic bag, cover it with a tea towel, and
   crush the crackers with a rolling pin. Transfer the crumbs to a
   medium bowl and stir in the melted butter and vanilla. Scrape the
   crust mixture into the prepared pan and firmly press it into the
   bottom and 1 inch up the sides, using your fingers. Place the crust
   in the freezer while you make the filling.

3. To make the filling, briefly beat the cream cheese on medium-low
   speed in the bowl of a stand mixer fitted with the paddle attachment, just until smooth, scraping the bowl with a flexible spatula
   as needed. Beat in the sweetened condensed milk and salt just
   until combined, and then the lemon juice and vanilla. Turn off
   the mixer as soon as all the ingredients are incorporated. Do
   not overmix or the cream cheese will lose structure. Scrape the
   filling into the prepared crust, smoothing the top with an offset
   spatula or butter knife. Cover the cheesecake with plastic wrap
   and refrigerate it for at least 5 hours, but preferably overnight.

4. When ready to serve, remove the sides of the pan and, if you would like to remove the base (though you don't have to), slide a long, serrated knife between the crust and the parchment paper and transfer the cake to a serving plate. Slice the cake with a large chef's knife that's been dipped in hot water and dried in between slices. Serve with a dusting of cocoa powder, if using. Keep the cake, wrapped, in the refrigerator for up to 3 days.

Vanilla Birthday Cupcakes with Chocolate Glaze

MAKES 18 CUPCAKES
ACTIVE TIME: 15 MINUTES
BAKING TIME: 18 TO 22 MINUTES

FOR THE CUPCAKES

⅔ cup (158 ml) vegetable oil
1 cup (200 g) granulated sugar
2½ teaspoons vanilla extract
2 large eggs
⅔ cup (158 ml) whole milk
1½ teaspoons baking powder
¾ teaspoon kosher salt
1½ cups (195 g) all-purpose flour

FOR THE GLAZE

4 ounces (113 g) semisweet
   chocolate chips
⅓ cup (79 ml) heavy cream
1 tablespoon light corn syrup
⅛ teaspoon kosher salt

Growing up, my b-day cake was always a mint–chocolate chip ice cream cake from Baskin Robbins. It didn't even matter that my b-day is in November (the 30th, to be exact, if you're interested in sending a card/gift, etc.), which isn't exactly ice cream cake season. *Now* on my birthday, my boys make me a cake from a boxed mix (as cakes from a box are my one true love), and these adorbs soft-crumbed, moist cups are my homemade nod to cake-mix cakes everywhere. They're glazed rather than frosted, because this is an easy-peasy baking book (in case you did not know) and glazed cups = easy-peasy to the max.

1. Heat the oven to 350°F. Line a 12-well muffin tin with paper liners (if you have two, line the second with 6 liners).

2. To make the cupcakes, whisk together the oil, sugar, and vanilla in a large bowl for 30 seconds. Whisk in the eggs, one at a time, and then the milk. Sprinkle the baking powder and salt into the bowl, one at a time, vigorously whisking after each. Gently fold in the flour with a flexible spatula just until the last streak disappears. The batter will be lumpy and thin.

3. Pour enough batter into each lined well so that they are two-thirds of the way full, then bake for 18 to 22 minutes, rotating the pan at the halfway point (if you are using two pans, swap their positions after rotating them). The cupcakes are done when a tester inserted into one comes out with a few moist crumbs.

4. Remove from the oven and let cool for about 5 minutes, or until you can safely remove the cupcakes from the tin without burning yourself. Let cool before glazing. Repeat with the remaining batter if using one tin, rinsing the pan in cold water to cool it, drying, and relining.

5. To make the glaze, combine all its ingredients in a small, microwave-safe bowl and microwave on HIGH for two or three 30-second bursts, stirring after each with a fork, until melted and smooth. Dip the top of each cupcake in the glaze, and let set for about 30 minutes before serving. Keep the cupcakes in an airtight container on the counter for up to 3 days.

CHAPTER 3.

For the Chocolate Lovers

I'm a chocolate lover, first and foremost, and although lots of the bakes in this book call for chocolate in some form or another ('cause . . . chocolate), in these particular recipes, chocolate is the main event (and sometimes appears in surprising ways, like in banana bread and carrot cake). I always call for Dutch-processed cocoa powder in my treats, as opposed to natural (for stronger color and flavor), as well as chocolate in the form of chips, as opposed to bars (for ease of use). However, the recipes will all work with either powder, as well as with chips or a chopped bar. And although all of these recipes are a cinch to assemble (natch), they actually satisfy all *different* kinds of chocolate cravings: if you're dreaming about candy, make Crispy Chocolate Crunch Bark (page 109)— and not just on Halloween, that's just when I tend to make it—or the White Chocolate "Cookie" Truffles (page 113). If you need chocolate *now*, make the Molten Double Chocolate Mug Cake (page 97). If you need it for breakfast (I mean, who doesn't?), make the Chocolate Crème Fraîche Banana Bread (page 88; yes, you can use sour cream—or even whole-milk yogurt) or the Deeply Chocolaty Baked Donuts with Buttermilk Glaze and Sprinkles (page 91). Finally, if you're craving a nostalgic treat that will give you loads of packaged snack-cake vibes (anyone remember Hostess Suzy Qs?), then make the "Shhh, Don't Tell!" Devil's Food Snacking Cake with Marshmallow Frosting (page 102). Seriously, there is something here for all of your chocolaty wants and needs.

Chocolate Crème Fraîche Banana Bread

ONE 8½-BY-4½-INCH LOAF CAKE

ACTIVE TIME: 10 MINUTES

BAKE TIME: 65 TO 70 MINUTES

Cooking spray or softened unsalted butter for pan

1¼ cups (162 g) all-purpose flour

½ cup (40 g) Dutch-processed cocoa powder

1 teaspoon baking soda

½ teaspoon kosher salt

¾ cup (127 g) semisweet chocolate chips

1 cup (200 g) granulated sugar

½ cup (118 ml) vegetable oil

1 teaspoon vanilla extract

1 large egg, at room temperature

¼ cup (57 g) crème fraîche, or sour cream

1 cup (230 g) mashed bananas, about 2 very ripe ones

Look, banana bread is good, but *chocolate* banana bread is even better. Here, the bread gets a little tang from the crème fraîche, which plays so nicely with the rich chocolate flavor. As do the bananas, since chocolate and 'nanas is a match made in fruit-and-chocolate heaven—particularly when both cocoa powder AND pockets of melted chips are in the mix. Oh, and did I mention that this most tasty of loaves is moist? Well, she is and she only gets better with age (as we all do, I like to think)—oil-based cakes are like that, and that's why I love them so.

1. Heat the oven to 350°F. Grease an 8-½-by-4½-inch loaf pan with cooking spray or softened butter. Line the bottom with a large sheet of parchment paper that extends up and over the two long sides of the pan (like a cradle for your cake).

2. Whisk together the flour, cocoa powder, baking soda, and salt in a medium bowl. Whisk in the chocolate chips. Whisk the sugar, oil, and vanilla in a large bowl for 30 seconds; whisk in the egg and then the crème fraîche, and finally the bananas. Gently fold the dry ingredients into the wet with a flexible spatula just until the last streak of flour disappears. Don't overmix.

3. Transfer the batter to the prepared pan and smooth the top. Bake for 65 to 70 minutes, rotating the pan at the halfway point. The bread is done when a wooden skewer inserted into the center comes out with a moist crumb or two.

4. Remove from the oven and let cool in the pan for about 20 minutes, or until you can safely lift the loaf out of the pan by the parchment overhang without burning yourself. Run a butter knife around the edges if it resists. Let cool to room temperature before serving. Keep the bread, wrapped, on the counter for up to 3 days.

Deeply Chocolaty Baked Donuts with Buttermilk Glaze and Sprinkles

MAKES 18 DONUTS (OR
18 MUFFINS, OR A LOT OF MINIS)
ACTIVE TIME: 15 MINUTES
BAKE TIME: 9 TO 11 MINUTES FOR
DONUTS AND MINI MUFFINS,
ABOUT 25 FOR STANDARD MUFFINS

Cooking spray or softened
unsalted butter for pan

FOR THE DONUTS

1¾ cups (227 g) all-purpose flour

¾ cup (60 g) Dutch-processed
cocoa powder

1 teaspoon baking powder

1 teaspoon baking soda

1 teaspoon kosher salt

¾ cup (127 g) semisweet chocolate
chips

½ cup (118 ml) vegetable oil

1⅓ cups packed (267 g) light brown
sugar

2 teaspoons vanilla extract

2 large eggs

⅔ cup (158 ml) buttermilk

**FOR THE GLAZE (MAKES
ENOUGH FOR TWO DIPS
PER DONUT)**

3 cups (360 g) confectioners' sugar

¼ cup plus 2 tablespoons (89 ml)
buttermilk

1½ teaspoons vanilla extract

1 teaspoon freshly squeezed lemon
juice

1 teaspoon kosher salt

Rainbow sprinkles for decorating

Any chance you're into super-soft and chocolaty donuts? Good, 'cause these are they. If you don't have a donut pan, use a muffin tin (¼ cup of batter per muffin) or a mini muffin pan (1 tablespoon of batter per mini well) for insanely cute donut holes.

———

1. Heat the oven to 350°F. Generously grease a donut pan (or a regular or mini muffin tin) with cooking spray or softened butter.

2. To make the donuts, whisk together the flour, cocoa powder, baking powder, baking soda, salt, and chocolate chips in a medium bowl. Whisk together the oil, brown sugar, and vanilla in a large bowl for 30 seconds; whisk in the eggs, one at a time, and then the buttermilk. Gently fold in the dry ingredients with a flexible spatula just until the last streak of flour disappears.

3. Fill the donut molds with ¼ cup (55 to 60 g) of batter, about three-quarters of the way full. You can do this by filling a resealable plastic bag with batter, snipping off one corner, and using it as a makeshift piping bag.

4. Bake for 9 to 11 minutes, rotating at the halfway point, until a wooden skewer inserted into a donut comes out clean and the donut springs back when you lightly press it. Remove from the oven and let cool for about 5 minutes, or until you can safely remove the donuts from the pan. Bring them to room temperature on a cooling rack set inside a baking sheet before glazing. Repeat with the remaining batter, rinsing the pan in cold water to cool it, drying, and regreasing it between rounds.

5. To make the glaze, whisk together the confectioners' sugar, buttermilk, vanilla, lemon juice, and salt in a small bowl, until thick yet pourable. If you need to adjust the consistency, add more buttermilk or more sugar as necessary. Dip one side of each donut in the glaze, letting it drip off before placing the donuts upright on the rack. Let set briefly before redipping. Decorate with rainbow sprinkles and let set for 15 minutes before enjoying. The donuts are best the day they are made, but will keep in an airtight container on the counter for up to 3 days.

Chewy, Fudgy Brownies

MAKES 16 BROWNIES
ACTIVE TIME: 10 MINUTES
BAKE TIME: 25 TO 30 MINUTES

Cooking spray or softened
  unsalted butter for pan
¾ cup (60 g) Dutch-processed
  cocoa powder
⅔ cup (87 g) all-purpose flour
1 teaspoon kosher salt
⅔ cup (113 g) semisweet chocolate chips
½ cup (113 g) unsalted butter
¼ cup (59 ml) vegetable oil
1 cup (200 g) granulated sugar
¼ cup (50 g) light brown sugar
1 tablespoon vanilla extract
2 large eggs, at room
  temperature

I really wanted to *call* these "Best Brownies Ever," but I know there are some who might take issue with that. So, instead, the name merely captures the two most important qualities *in* the best brownies ever: fudginess and chewiness (sorry, my cakey acquaintances). When developing these, I was looking to replicate the "boxed brownie" flavor and texture of my dreams (and that coveted crinkly top—which occurs when sugar is melted in a warm mixture of butter and chocolate) and I *think* I achieved it, so, yes, celebrations are in order and all of that. But whether your dreams are boxed brownie related or not, I'm pretty sure you do not want to miss out on a snackable bake that answers to the name "best ever," you feel me? And I like room temp eggs here, but if you forget to take them out of the fridge; see page 17 for how to warm 'em up quickly.

1. Heat the oven to 350°F. Grease an 8-inch square cake pan with cooking spray or softened butter. Line the bottom with a large sheet of parchment paper that extends up and over two opposite sides of the pan.

2. Whisk together the cocoa powder, flour, salt, and ⅓ cup (56 g) of the chocolate chips in a small bowl. Microwave the remaining ⅓ cup (56 g) chips, butter, and oil in a large microwave-safe bowl on HIGH in three 30-second bursts, whisking after each, until melted, smooth, and quite warm (I mean, you don't want to boil it, but the warmer it is, the easier it will be for the sugars to melt when you add them). Immediately whisk the granulated and brown sugars into the warm chocolate mixture. Working relatively quickly, so as to keep the mixture warm, whisk in the vanilla and then the eggs, very gently. Fold the dry ingredients into the wet with a flexible spatula just until the last streak of flour disappears. Don't overmix.

3. Scrape the batter into the prepared pan and bake for 25 to 28 minutes, rotating the pan at the halfway point. The brownies are ready when a cake tester comes out with a few moist, almost wet, crumbs—do not overbake.

4. Remove from the oven. Let cool until room temperature and then lift the brownies out of the pan by the parchment overhang. Run a butter knife around the edges if there's resistance. Slice into 16 squares and serve. Keep the brownies in an airtight container on the counter for up to 3 days, but they are fantastic frozen and nibbled straight from the freezer.

Chocolate Grasshopper Whoopie Pies with Minty Green Buttercream

MAKES 15 PIES
ACTIVE TIME: 20 MINUTES
BAKE TIME: 8 TO 9 MINUTES

FOR THE WHOOPIES

⅔ cup (53 g) Dutch-processed cocoa powder

½ cup (118 ml) very hot tap water

1 teaspoon espresso powder (optional)

1 cup packed (200 g) light brown sugar

½ cup (118 ml) vegetable oil

2 teaspoons vanilla extract

1 large egg

¼ cup (59 ml) buttermilk

1 teaspoon baking soda

½ teaspoon baking powder

½ teaspoon kosher salt

1¾ cups (227 g) all-purpose flour

FOR THE BUTTERCREAM

½ cup (113 g) unsalted butter, at room temperature

½ teaspoon peppermint extract

¼ teaspoon kosher salt

2 cups (240 g) confectioners' sugar

2 to 3 tablespoons heavy cream, at room temperature

1 to 2 drops green food coloring

Green sparkling sugar for decorating

Whoopie pies were my favorite thing to make and eat when I worked at Baked, the bakery where the magic (okay, *my* magic) first happened. I liked them better than their (world-famous) cupcakes due to the excellent cake-to-filling ratio. I mean, with whoopies, there is never too little frosting and never too much cake: they are just perfect that way. Also, the whoopie "cookies" themselves are easily assembled in a single bowl and bake in less than 10 minutes. Amazing, I know.

1. Heat the oven to 350°F. Have ready two parchment-lined baking sheets.

2. To make the whoopies, whisk together the cocoa powder, water, and espresso powder (if using) in a glass liquid measuring cup or small bowl and set aside. Whisk together the brown sugar, oil, and vanilla in a large bowl for 30 seconds; whisk in the egg and then the buttermilk, then sprinkle the baking powder, baking soda, and salt into the bowl, one at a time, vigorously whisking after each. Fold half of the flour into the bowl with a flexible spatula, followed by the cocoa powder mixture, and then the other half of the flour. Fold just until the last streak of flour disappears. Don't overmix.

3. Scoop 1½ tablespoons of batter, using a portion scoop or measuring spoons, evenly placing 12 on each prepared baking sheet. Bake for 8 to 9 minutes, rotating and swapping the placement of the sheets at the halfway point, until the pies are dry to the touch and bounce back when lightly pressed. Remove from the oven and let cool completely on the pans before filling. Repeat with any remaining batter.

VARIATIONS

For Peppermint Whoopie Pies, substitute red food coloring for the green and roll the just-filled pies in crushed candy canes or red starlight mints, rather than green sparkling sugar. For Double Chocolate Malted Whoopie Pies, replace the mint green buttercream with a double batch of the Chocolate Malted Cream Cheese Frosting (page 50) and roll the just-filled pies in crushed malted milk balls.

4. To make the buttercream, beat together the butter, peppermint extract, and salt on medium-low speed in the bowl of a stand mixer fitted with the paddle attachment, until smooth. Beat in the confectioners' sugar, ½ cup (60 g) at a time, alternating with splashes of the cream, scraping the bowl with a flexible spatula, as needed. Add the food coloring, a drop at a time, until you achieve green nirvana, and beat for an additional 3 minutes on medium speed, until light and fluffy. Turn half of the pies upside down, top with about 1½ tablespoons of filling, and cover with an upturned pie, pressing gently. Place the green sparkling sugar in a shallow bowl and roll the edges of the just-filled pies in the sugar and serve. Keep the whoopies in an airtight container on the counter for up to 3 days.

Molten Double Chocolate Mug Cake

MAKES ABOUT 2 SERVINGS,
IF YOU ARE INTO SHARING,
ONLY 1 IF YOU ARE NOT
(THAT'D BE ME—THE OG HATER
OF SHARING)

ACTIVE TIME: 2 MINUTES
MICROWAVE TIME: 2 MINUTES

3 tablespoons vegetable oil

¼ cup (50 g) granulated sugar

1 large egg yolk

½ teaspoon vanilla extract

3 tablespoons sour cream

½ teaspoon baking powder

¼ teaspoon kosher salt

3 tablespoons all-purpose flour

2 tablespoons Dutch-processed cocoa powder

3 tablespoons semisweet chocolate chips

Vanilla ice cream for serving

No one ever says, when looking at a mug cake, "Why, that's the prettiest thing I've ever seen." But extremely yummy cakes (and a cookie!) in less than 2 minutes do have their price (and looks aren't everything, in case you did not get the memo). Yes, these mug cakes call for yolks and I know that separating eggs is no one's idea of a good time. While a whole egg in a mug cake makes it rise high, which we all love, it also makes it taste like rubber, which we don't love. And you can use the leftover egg white in a batch of Straight-Up Coconut Macaroons (page 124), so there's that, too. Finally, a word to the mug-cake-making wise: the size of your mug and the strength of your microwave will both impact the success of your cake/cookie. Using a 12- to 14-ounce ceramic mug guarantees no overflowing of cake in *my* microwave, but if yours is all-powerful, consider preparing and microwaving yours in a cereal bowl for assurance.

Stir together the oil and sugar in a 12- or 14-ounce ceramic, microwave-safe mug, using a fork. Stir in the egg yolk and vanilla, and then the sour cream. Stir in the baking powder and salt, and then the flour and cocoa powder. Stir in the chocolate chips and microwave on HIGH for 1 to 2 minutes, depending on your microwave (in my microwave, 1½ minutes is just about golden). The cake is done when it rises above the edge of the mug (or close to it) and its top looks glossy and set, but not wet. Let cool briefly—it will collapse—sorry, but true. The center will be more moltenlike than cakelike, very soft, and very hot—be careful! Enjoy ASAP with vanilla ice cream.

VARIATIONS

For Molten Rainbow Sprinkle Mug Cake, substitute 2 tablespoons of all-purpose flour for the cocoa powder and 1 tablespoon of rainbow sprinkles for the chocolate chips. For Molten Chocolate Chip Cookie Mug Cake, substitute 3 tablespoons of light brown sugar for the granulated; omit the sour cream; and substitute 1½ tablespoons of all-purpose flour for the cocoa powder and a rounded ¼ teaspoon of baking soda for the baking powder. Microwave on HIGH for 1 to 1½ minutes, depending on your microwave. A 10-ounce ceramic, microwave-safe mug should work here.

Flourless Chocolate (Weeknight) Dinner Party Cake

MAKES ONE 8-INCH ROUND CAKE
ACTIVE TIME: 5 MINUTES
BAKE TIME: 30 TO 35 MINUTES

Cooking spray or softened unsalted butter for pan
1 cup (226 g) unsalted butter
1½ cups (255 g) semisweet chocolate chips
1⅓ cups packed (266 g) light brown sugar
2 teaspoons vanilla extract
¾ teaspoon kosher salt
6 large eggs, at room temperature
Crème fraîche for serving

I call this a weeknight dinner party cake because there is no other that is as simple and as elegant. But it could just as easily be called straight-up dinner party cake or after-school cake (though those would be some crazy lucky kids who got to eat a sliver of this before soccer practice). I did not set out to make a flourless cake when I developed it years ago, but merely an easy one that showcased chocolate in all its glory. Originally inspired by Molly Wizenberg's fantastic Winning Hearts and Minds Cake, the texture is almost like a rich, dense pudding and is deeelish with a dollop of crème fraîche. Oh, and frozen slivers are super yum, too.

1. Heat the oven to 375°F. Grease an 8-inch round cake pan with cooking spray or softened butter. Line the bottom with parchment paper.

2. Microwave the butter and chocolate together in a large, microwave-safe bowl on HIGH in 30-second bursts, stirring after each with a flexible spatula until melted and smooth. Off the heat, whisk in the brown sugar, vanilla, salt, and then the eggs, very gently and one at a time. Scrape the batter into the prepared pan and bake for 30 to 35 minutes, rotating the pan at the halfway point. The cake is ready when its top is crackly, its edges are puffed, and the center wobbles just a bit.

3. Remove from the oven and let cool for about 10 minutes; the cake will collapse a little. Carefully run a butter knife around its edges and invert the cake onto a cooling rack, right side up. Let cool to room temperature before serving slices with a dollop of crème fraîche. Keep the cake, wrapped, on the counter for up to 3 days and it will last for up to a month frozen (and frozen slivers + TV-indulging = fire. And fire is a good thing, in case you do not live with teenagers and so do not know).

Chocolate Carrot Sheet Cake with Cream Cheese Glaze

ONE 9-BY-13-INCH
RECTANGULAR CAKE
ACTIVE TIME: 20 MINUTES
BAKE TIME: 40 TO 45 MINUTES

Cooking spray or softened
  unsalted butter for pan

FOR THE CAKE

1½ cups (195 g) all-purpose flour

¾ cup (60 g) Dutch-processed
  cocoa powder

2¼ teaspoons baking powder

½ teaspoon baking soda

1 teaspoon kosher salt

2 cups (400 g) granulated sugar

1 cup (237 ml) vegetable oil

2 teaspoons vanilla extract

4 large eggs

½ cup (118 ml) whole milk

3 cups lightly packed, finely
  grated carrots (6 to
  7 carrots; 285 g)

FOR THE GLAZE

4 ounces (113 g) cream cheese,
  at room temperature

½ cup plus 2 tablespoons (75 g)
  confectioners' sugar

¼ teaspoon kosher salt

2½ tablespoons whole milk

¾ teaspoon vanilla extract

A drop or two of orange food
  coloring, or 1 drop red + 1 drop
  yellow (optional, but festive)

Orange sparkling sugar for
  decorating

Here's the thing about this chocolate cake: no one will ever know there are carrots in it (except for you, because you were the one who grated them all) unless you tell them. Yes, they add wonderful—mysterious—moisture and texture to this fudgy and soft-crumbed cake, but carrot flavor (or color)? Nope. I like to tint the glaze a pale orange and sprinkle it with orange sparkling sugar, as a nod to the carrots, but you do you (as I know you will . . .). And I like finely grated carrots here, as they literally melt into the cake, but if grating carrots on a Microplane does not sound like a good time to you, feel free to grate them on the large holes of a box grater.

1. Heat the oven to 350°F. Grease a 9-by-13-inch pan with cooking spray or softened butter. Line the bottom with a sheet of parchment paper (you won't be removing the cake from the pan, so no need for a parchment paper "cradle").

2. To make the cake, whisk together the flour, cocoa powder, baking powder, baking soda, and salt in a medium bowl. Whisk together the granulated sugar, oil, and vanilla in a large bowl for 30 seconds; whisk in the eggs, one at a time, and then the milk. Gently fold the dry ingredients into the wet with a flexible spatula just until a few streaks of flour remain. Fold in the carrots.

3. Scrape the batter into the prepared pan and bake for 40 to 45 minutes, rotating the cake at the halfway point. The cake is done when a wooden skewer inserted into the center comes out with a moist crumb or two. Remove from the oven and let cool to room temperature in the pan before glazing.

4. To make the glaze, gently whisk together (so as not to send sugar flying around your kitchen) the cream cheese, confectioners' sugar, and salt in a medium bowl until combined and then vigorously whisk until smooth. Whisk in the milk, vanilla, and food coloring (if using), then spread the glaze decoratively over the cooled cake. Sprinkle with the orange sparkling sugar. Chill for about 15 minutes in the refrigerator to set the glaze before slicing and serving. Keep the cake, wrapped in the pan, in the refrigerator for up to 3 days.

"Shhh, Don't Tell!" Devil's Food Snacking Cake with Marshmallow Frosting

MAKES ONE 8-INCH SQUARE
CAKE
ACTIVE TIME: 20 MINUTES
BAKING TIME: 25 TO 30 MINUTES

Cooking spray or softened
  unsalted butter for pan

FOR THE CAKE
1 cup (237 ml) very hot tap water
½ cup (40 g) Dutch-processed
  cocoa powder
1 teaspoon espresso powder
  (optional)
¾ cup (150 g) full-fat mayonnaise
1 cup (200 g) granulated sugar
1½ teaspoons vanilla extract
1 large egg
1 teaspoon baking powder
⅛ teaspoon baking soda
½ teaspoon kosher salt
1½ cups (195 g) all-purpose flour

FOR THE FROSTING
¾ cup (170 g) unsalted butter,
  at room temperature
7 ounces (198 g) marshmallow
  crème
1 tablespoon vanilla extract
½ teaspoon kosher salt
¾ cup (90 g) confectioners' sugar

Pink sparkling sugar for decorating (pink because it's my
  everything, but you do you)

Okay, now don't freak out, but there is mayonnaise in this cake. I know: crazy. But it takes the place of the oil in the recipe, as well as the eggs (though, yes, I do throw in one, for good measure). And the texture is so perfect, as well as the flavor, that you need to put any mayo-phobias behind you and get baking. The marshmallow frosting here is epic, but if you're just not feeling like pulling out your stand mixer for it, I totally understand and suggest you glaze this cutie with Cream Cheese Glaze (page 80) instead.

1. Heat the oven to 350°F. Grease an 8-inch square cake pan with cooking spray or softened butter. Line with a large sheet of parchment paper that extends up and over two opposite sides of the pan.

2. To make the cake, whisk together the water, cocoa powder, and espresso powder (if using) in a 2-cup glass measuring cup and set aside. Whisk together the mayonnaise, granulated sugar, and vanilla in a large bowl for 30 seconds; whisk in the egg. Sprinkle the baking powder, baking soda, and salt into the bowl, one at a time, vigorously whisking after each. Whisk half of the flour into the bowl, followed by the cocoa mixture, and then the other half of the flour. The batter will be thin.

3. Scrape the batter into the prepared pan and bake for 25 to 30 minutes, rotating the pan at the halfway point. The cake is ready when a wooden skewer inserted into the center comes out with a moist crumb or two. Remove from the oven and let cool in the pan for about 20 minutes, or until you can safely lift the cake out by the parchment overhang without burning yourself. Run a butter knife around the edges if it resists. Let cool to room temperature before frosting.

4. To make the frosting, beat together the butter, marshmallow crème, vanilla, and salt on medium speed in the bowl of a stand mixer fitted with the paddle attachment until fluffy, 1 to 2 minutes, scraping the bowl with a flexible spatula, as needed. Beat in the confectioners' sugar. Increase the speed to medium-high

and continue to beat for 2 to 3 minutes until light and fluffy. Generously frost the cake, sprinkle with sparkling sugar, and serve.

5. Keep the cake, wrapped, on the counter for up to 3 days—and FYI, she is an excellent traveler, and does very well in hot weather (basically, she's a dream).

Black Bottom Cupcakes with Cream Cheese Filling

MAKES 12 CUPCAKES
ACTIVE TIME: 15 MINUTES
BAKE TIME: 22 TO 25 MINUTES

FOR THE FILLING

6 ounces (170 g) cream cheese, at room temperature

3 tablespoons packed light brown sugar

½ teaspoon kosher salt

1 large egg

1 teaspoon vanilla extract

3 tablespoons semisweet chocolate chips, finely chopped

FOR THE CUPCAKES

1 cup (130 g) all-purpose flour

¼ cup plus 2 tablespoons (30 g) Dutch-processed cocoa powder

¾ teaspoon baking powder

½ teaspoon baking soda

½ teaspoon kosher salt

1 cup packed (200 g) light brown sugar

¼ cup (59 ml) vegetable oil

1½ teaspoons vanilla extract

1 large egg

1 cup very hot tap water

1 teaspoon espresso powder (optional)

Gosh, am I ever into these cups. I mean the legendary combo of chocolate and cream cheese is so good, and yet so weirdly underrated. Here, the softest and most perfect of chocolate cakes surrounds the tastiest little tangy pocket of sweetened cream cheese, studded with melted chocolaty bits. I like serving them a little warm when the creamy middles are still just this side of molten.

1. Heat the oven to 350°F. Have ready a 12-well muffin tin lined with paper liners.

2. To make the filling, stir together the cream cheese, brown sugar, and salt with a fork in a medium bowl until combined. Gently stir in the egg and vanilla as you don't want to overmix, and then the chocolate. Refrigerate while you make the cupcake batter.

3. To make the cupcakes, whisk together the flour, cocoa powder, baking powder, baking soda, salt, and brown sugar in a large bowl. Whisk together the oil, vanilla, and egg in a liquid glass measuring cup and pour over the dry ingredients. Using the same measuring cup, measure the water, whisk in the espresso powder (if using), and pour into the bowl, as well. Whisk the batter until smooth. It will be very thin. Don't worry.

4. Evenly portion the batter among the prepared muffin wells. Top each with 1½ tablespoons of cream cheese filling, using a small portion scoop or measuring spoons.

5. Bake for 22 to 25 minutes, rotating the pan at the halfway point, until a wooden skewer inserted on the side of the cupcake comes out with a moist crumb. Remove from the oven and let cool for about 5 minutes, or until you can safely remove the cupcakes from the tin without burning yourself. Serve the cups warm (for a pleasantly gooey experience) or at room temperature. Keep the cupcakes in an airtight container in the refrigerator for up to 3 days.

Easiest-Peasiest Chocolate Marshmallow Mousse

MAKES 6 INDIVIDUAL MOUSSES
ACTIVE TIME: 10 MINUTES
INACTIVE TIME: 45 TO 60 MINUTES

3 cups (130 g) mini marshmallows

2 cups (474 ml) heavy cream

1 cup (170 g) semisweet chocolate chips

1 tablespoon Dutch-processed cocoa powder

1 teaspoon espresso powder (optional)

½ teaspoon kosher salt

2 teaspoons vanilla extract

Extremely Special Whipped Cream (page 230) for serving

Marshies are the true heroes in this mousse (and in life), giving it its ethereal texture and allowing you to skip any egg white whipping or gelatin blooming. In other words, simple-sweet-time to the max. Funnily enough, though, the marshmallows here don't impart any specific flavor. Instead, they are a savvy and deeply respected backroom player. The lucky chums with whom you share the mousse won't even know they're marshies in the mix, and I won't tell, if you don't.

1. Have ready six 6-ounce ramekins or teacups.

2. Place the marshmallows, ¾ cup (177 ml) of the cream, and the chocolate, cocoa powder, espresso powder (if using), and salt in a medium saucepan over medium heat and cook until the marshmallows melt and the mixture is smooth, stirring frequently with a flexible spatula. Scrape into a large bowl and let cool to room temp in the refrigerator, or rest the bowl in a larger bowl filled with some ice on the counter and whisk periodically.

3. Whisk the remaining 1¼ cups (296 ml) of cream and vanilla on medium to medium-high speed in the bowl of a stand mixer fitted with the whisk attachment until medium to stiff peaks form. Gently fold the cream into the cooled chocolate mixture in three additions.

4. Transfer to the six ramekins and serve immediately with *Extremely* Special Whipped Cream, or refrigerate until chilled, 45 to 60 minutes. Keep the mousse, wrapped, in the refrigerator for up to 4 days.

Crispy Chocolate Crunch Bark

MAKES ABOUT ¾ POUND
OF BARK
ACTIVE TIME: 5 MINUTES
INACTIVE TIME: 30 TO 60
MINUTES

Cooking spray or softened
unsalted butter for pan

2 cups (340 g) milk chocolate
chips

2 tablespoons vegetable
shortening

½ teaspoon kosher salt

2½ cups (71 g) crispy rice cereal,
such as Rice Krispies

Flaky sea salt for sprinkling

This bark is my take on an extra-crispy and slightly thicker Nestlé Crunch bar. I love recipes like this one because, when I was first developing it, I was like, "Oh, this might be good." And then after I actually made it, tasted it, and watched my (critical, but lovely) husband eat almost my entire frozen stash, I realized I had actually created something *fantastic*. I think of this as Halloween bark, only because I sought out mini Nestlé Crunch bars with a vengeance as a child when trick-or-treating (and, yes, over the years, I've been known to steal them, along with Reese's Peanut Butter Cups, from my own sleeping children's treat bags). But you can think of it however you would like, as long as you make it frequently for the NCB fans in *your* life.

1. Grease an 8-inch square cake pan with cooking spray or softened butter and line with a long sheet of parchment that extends up and over two opposite sides of the pan.

2. Microwave the chocolate, shortening, and kosher salt together on HIGH in a large, microwave-safe bowl in two 30-second bursts, stirring after each with a flexible spatula, or until melted and smooth. Fold in the cereal and immediately scrape the mixture into the prepared pan, evenly spreading it across the bottom. Sprinkle with the flaky sea salt and place in the refrigerator for about an hour to firm up, or in the freezer for a half an hour.

3. Once firm, lift the bark from the pan by the parchment over-hang, running a butter knife around the edges if it resists, and crack it into jagged pieces for serving—or cut up into 16 nice little squares if you're feeling fancy. Keep the bark in an airtight container on the counter for up to a week, or, if your kitchen is warm, store in the refrigerator or freezer.

TikTok for Life

In the early winter of 2020, some food media pals suggested I make some TikTok videos with them. I hadn't a clue as to what that entailed, but because I pride myself on embracing *all* the opportunities that come my way, saying no wasn't really an option. We decided that we'd shoot two videos—one in which I demoed my World's Best Rice Krispies Treats and one in which I made my Chocolate Marshmallow Walnut Fudge with Flaky Sea Salt. Needless to say, when I told my younger son that I'd be making "tock-tick" videos in the next few weeks, he was unimpressed. That March, I showed up in the studio to shoot the videos and asked if they were looking for me to do anything in particular when making my treats. "Talk fast" was the only direction I was given. And so, I did. But in hindsight, it was more than fast, as I also just kind of went a little bananas as one is wont to do when TikToking. Both videos went viral, with over 1 million views shortly thereafter, so I guess you could say I had done something right. Although my media pals and I made plans to partner on many more tock-ticks, the world kind of shut down a few weeks after we shot my first two and so I was forced to go full-steam ahead solo, and at home. And the rest is history. My following grew, the wackiness continued, until it didn't (as all that fast and loud talking day in and day out can be exhausting). Now my videos are only a little fast and a lot funny ('cause I'm a little fast and a lot funny) and that seems to work for everyone. TikTok is a very different platform now than it was when I first started there, but I have a weakness for it, despite the notoriously fickle viewers. I love making sweets and I'm a little quirky, and that combo still has TikTok written all over it.

White Chocolate "Cookie" Truffles

MAKES ABOUT 20 TRUFFLES
ACTIVE TIME: 15 MINUTES
INACTIVE TIME: 15 MINUTES

4 ounces (113 g) cream cheese, at room temperature

½ teaspoon kosher salt

¾ teaspoon vanilla extract

18 cream-filled chocolate sandwich cookies, such as Oreo® (200 g), from half of a 14-ounce package

2 cups (340 g) white chocolate chips

2 tablespoons vegetable oil

I would never have even known that such a thing as a white chocolate "cookie" truffle existed (traditionally made with everyone's favorite cream-filled chocolate sandwich cookie, the Oreo®) if not for my beloved TikTok (sorry, haters). I learned about it on the app and have never looked back. Who knew one could have so much tasty fun with a cream-filled chocolate sandwich cookie or two (or 18)? You may have a little extra melted white chocolate after truffle dipping, so might I suggest using it as a fondue for a salty pretzel or two? Some potato chips? A Dorito? As all of these salty treats would be extra yum with a little melted white chocolate.

1. Have ready a parchment-lined baking sheet.

2. Combine the cream cheese, salt, and vanilla in a large bowl, using a fork. Seal the cookies in a resealable plastic bag, cover the bag with a tea towel, and crush the cookies with a rolling pin until fine crumbs form. Or you can grind them in a food processor. Remove 2 tablespoons of the crumbs for decorating and transfer the remaining crumbs to the cream cheese mixture and, with a flexible spatula, stir until thoroughly combined. Scoop the mixture, using a 1-tablespoon portion scoop or a measuring spoon, and roll into balls with your hands. Place the truffle balls on the prepared baking sheet and freeze for 15 minutes.

3. Microwave the chocolate and oil in a medium, microwave-safe bowl on HIGH in two 30-second bursts, stirring after each until the chocolate melts. Drop each truffle into the chocolate, one at a time, lifting each one out with a fork or slotted spoon and allowing the excess to drip off. Place the dipped truffles back on the baking sheet and immediately sprinkle each one with a tiny bit of crumbs. Rewarm the chocolate in the microwave if it hardens up while you work, and if a little chocolate pools around the bottom of your truffles, you can chill them briefly and, using a paring knife, trim away the excess. Serve the truffles at room temperature.

4. Keep the truffles in an airtight container in the refrigerator for up to a week.

CHAPTER 4. # Nuts for Nuts

Nuts are a wonderful way to add flavor and texture to snackable bakes, and I put them in everything from granola to cake to blondies to muffins (to straight into my mouth, by the handful). But I'll admit it: I use the word "nut" a little loosely here, as I also include recipes calling for coconut in this chapter (because it is kind of a fruit/tree-nut hybrid and has the word "nut" in its name—and that counts for something, no?). And I include tahini, which is really sesame paste (because seeds and nuts are pals and also because when you combine tahini with chocolate it is glorious—hello, Tahini Milk Chocolate Bars, page 127). But, if you're not as nutty as I am, and you like the idea of chocolate buns, but not *pistachio* chocolate buns, leave them out—I won't have hurt feelings (same goes for the hazelnuts in the granola, and the pecans in the blondies and muffins). Finally, if a recipe calls for toasting the nuts, please do so until they are *deeply* toasted (meaning they have truly darkened in color and are quite fragrant) for the nuttiest of flavors and the crunchiest of textures. See page 17 for instructions on toasting 101.

Pistachio Chocolate Anytime Buns

MAKES 12 BUNS
ACTIVE TIME: 15 MINUTES
BAKE TIME: 25 TO 30 MINUTES

Cooking spray or softened
   unsalted butter for pan

FOR THE FILLING
¼ cup (56 g) unsalted butter,
   melted and cooled slightly
¾ cup (150 g) light brown sugar
2 tablespoons Dutch-processed
   cocoa powder
½ teaspoon kosher salt
¼ teaspoon almond extract
   (optional, but encouraged)

FOR THE BUNS
2¼ cups (295 g) all-purpose flour,
   plus more for dusting
3 tablespoons light brown sugar
1 tablespoon baking powder
¼ teaspoon baking soda
1 teaspoon kosher salt
½ cup (113 g) unsalted butter, cold
   and cubed
⅔ cup (158 ml) whole milk

¼ cup (34 g) shelled roasted pis-
   tachios, salted or not, finely
   chopped
¼ cup (43 g) semisweet chocolate
   chips, finely chopped
1 cup (200g) granulated sugar for
   tossing

Ready for the easiest ever, but still mind-bogglingly delish, cinnamon roll–like anytime buns? Good, 'cause here they are. The dough is akin to a biscuit dough, so no need for yeast, or anything fussy like that. I like baking these in a muffin tin, à la Violet Bakery, rather than in a round cake pan, and if you pop them in a bowl of sugar immediately postbake, and enjoy them warm, you are in for the flakiest, butteriest, and choco-latiest little bun you ever did have. Oh, and the little smidge of almond extract here really helps pop the pistachio flavor, FYI.

1. Heat the oven to 350°F. Generously grease a 12-well muffin tin with cooking spray or softened butter.

2. To make the filling, stir the butter, brown sugar, cocoa powder, salt, and almond extract (if using) with a fork in a small bowl until combined.

3. To make the buns, whisk together the flour, brown sugar, baking powder, baking soda, and salt in a large bowl. Rub the butter into the flour mixture with your fingers until the butter is crumbly and pea-sized. Stir in the milk with a fork until combined.

4. Turn out the dough onto a generously floured work surface and knead it once or twice. Roll it into a rectangle, with the long side nearest you. Fold the two short ends into the center of the rectangle, one at a time, overlapping them, as you would when folding a letter. Rotate the rectangle so the long side is again nearest you, roll out the rectangle, and repeat the folds twice more, for a total of three complete letter folds. Roll the dough into a 9-by-12-inch rectangle.

5. Spread the filling over the dough, leaving a ½-inch border at the edges. Evenly sprinkle the nuts and chips over the filling, pressing them down lightly with your hands to adhere. Starting from the long edge of the rectangle nearest you, begin tightly rolling up the dough until a log is formed. Pinch the dough with your fingers to seal the seam. Cut the dough into 12 equal pieces and place them in the prepared muffin wells. Bake for 25 to 30 minutes, until the tops of the buns are lightly browned and a wooden skewer inserted into one comes out clean.

6. Pour the granulated sugar into a shallow bowl. Remove the tin from the oven and immediately (and carefully!) remove the buns from the tin—as their bottoms may stick if they rest in the tin too long—by running a butter knife around their edges and gently pulling them out with your fingers; if they stick at all on the bottom, just scrape out the stuck bit and press it back into your bun. Toss the buns in the sugar. Serve warm. The buns are best served the day they are made.

Coconut Hazelnut Granola with Olive Oil and Sesame Seeds

MAKES ABOUT 5 CUPS
ACTIVE TIME: 5 MINUTES
BAKE TIME: 45 MINUTES

¾ cup (177 ml) pure maple syrup

½ cup (118 g) extra-virgin olive oil

¼ cup (50 g) light brown sugar

1 teaspoon vanilla extract

1 teaspoon kosher salt

3 cups (300 g) quick 1-minute oats

1½ cups (202 g) whole hazelnuts, skinless

¼ cup (30 g) white sesame seeds

1 cup (45 g) unsweetened coconut flakes

Flaky sea salt for sprinkling

Are you team clumpy-granola, by any chance? You know, the kind of granola that you *snack on* (i.e., eat out of hand) 'cause it's less like a loose cereal and more like broken-up pieces of a Nature Valley granola bar? Yes? Okay, then have I got a granola for you. The secret is the quick oats that the recipe calls for, as they clump together like nobody's business during the bake. However, if clumpy isn't your thing, no worries: clumps can be broken—I promise. The recipe is inspired by my early days at Baked as a junior baker—okay, granola-packager, as when I first started, that was the only task with which they trusted me—because their granola, with hazelnuts *and* almonds, is some of the best I've ever had. If you cannot find skinless hazelnuts, toast yours on a baking sheet in a 350°F oven for 10 to 15 minutes, until they are lightly browned. Carefully wrap the warm nuts in a clean tea towel and rub them until their skins slip off. Ta-da!!!

1. Heat the oven to 325°F. Line a baking sheet with a nonstick mat, such as Silpat®, if you have one, or parchment paper.

2. Whisk together the maple syrup, oil, brown sugar, vanilla, and kosher salt in a large bowl. Fold in the oats, hazelnuts, and sesame seeds (but not the coconut), until all the dry ingredients are coated with the wet. Evenly spread the mixture on the prepared baking sheet and bake for about 45 minutes, rotating the pan and gently stirring after 20 minutes. Sprinkle on the coconut during the last 10 minutes of baking. The granola is ready when it has darkened in color and is wonderfully fragrant.

3. Remove from the oven and immediately sprinkle with the flaky sea salt. Let sit until the granola hardens and cools, then transfer to an airtight container, breaking up the myriad clumps (you're welcome), while doing so (pro tip: if you keep the clumps large, they're like mini granola bars for—you guessed it—*snacking*). Keep the granola in an airtight container on the counter for up to a month.

Pecan Coffeecake Muffins

MAKES 12 MUFFINS

ACTIVE TIME: 15 MINUTES

BAKING TIME: 22 TO 25 MINUTES

FOR THE TOPPING

¼ cup (33 g) all-purpose flour

¼ cup packed (50 g) light brown sugar

⅛ teaspoon kosher salt

2 tablespoons unsalted butter, melted and cooled

½ cup (56 g) pecans, finely chopped

FOR THE FILLING

¼ cup plus 2 tablespoons packed (75 g) light brown sugar

1½ teaspoons ground cinnamon

FOR THE MUFFINS

½ cup (118 ml) vegetable oil

¾ cup (150 g) granulated sugar

1 teaspoon vanilla extract

2 large eggs

½ cup (115 g) sour cream

½ teaspoon baking powder

¼ teaspoon baking soda

½ teaspoon kosher salt

1½ cups (195 g) all-purpose flour

I don't know about you, but coffeecake is my everything, and if a brown sugar filling and some finely chopped pecans are involved, all the better. Here, I've gone in the coffeecake *muffin* direction 'cause, in my book, individual cakes are the epitome of cute. But I'm thinking this might work as a snacking cake, too, if you added a few minutes to the bake time. Yes, these cuties have three components, as any coffeecake worth its weight in crumb topping does, but I'm not sure the filling even counts as a "component," as all you need to do to assemble it is whisk some sugar, cinnamon, and pecans together. Toasting the pecans for the filling elevates the flavor a bit, but if this reads too fussy to you, feel free to skip it.

1. Heat the oven to 350°F. Line a 12-well muffin tin with paper liners.

2. To make the topping, whisk together the flour, brown sugar, and salt in a small bowl. Stir in the melted butter with a fork, and then ¼ cup (28 g) of the pecans, and continue to stir until clumpy. Refrigerate while you make the filling and the muffins.

3. To make the filling, toast the remaining pecans, if you are so inclined (but no pressure), and whisk together the brown sugar, cinnamon, and (toasted?) pecans in a small bowl.

4. To make the muffins, whisk together the oil, granulated sugar, and vanilla in a large bowl for 30 seconds. Whisk in the eggs, and then the sour cream. Sprinkle the baking powder, baking soda, and salt into the bowl, one at a time, vigorously whisking after each. Gently fold in the flour with a flexible spatula, just until the last streak disappears. Don't overmix.

5. Divide half of the batter among the prepared muffin wells, about 1½ tablespoons for each, spreading it evenly over the bottom of the liners. Evenly top with the filling, a little less than a tablespoon for each muffin, pressing it down lightly with your fingers. Top with the rest of the batter, spreading it over the filling to cover. Finally, evenly divide the topping among the muffins, sprinkling about a tablespoon over each, and lightly press the mixture into the batter with your fingers.

Bake for 22 to 25 minutes, rotating the tin at the halfway point. The muffins are done when a wooden skewer inserted into the center of one comes out with a moist crumb or two and the crumb topping looks browned and crispy.

6. Remove from the oven and let cool for about 5 minutes, or until you can safely remove the muffins from the tin without burning yourself. Serve warm or at room temperature. Keep the muffins in an airtight container on the counter for up to 3 days.

Contest-Winning (Jumbo) Peanut Butter Cookies

MAKES 16 COOKIES
ACTIVE TIME: 5 MINUTES
BAKE TIME: 14 TO 16 MINUTES

¼ cup (48 g) vegetable shortening

¾ cup (169 g) unsalted butter, melted and cooled slightly

1½ cups packed (300 g) light brown sugar

1 tablespoon vanilla extract

2 large eggs, cold

1 cup (255 g) smooth peanut butter, not all-natural

1 teaspoon baking soda

¼ teaspoon baking powder

1¼ teaspoons kosher salt

2½ cups (325 g) all-purpose flour

1 cup (200 g) granulated sugar for rolling

Flaky sea salt for sprinkling

VARIATION

For Contest-Winning (Jumbo) Peanut Butter Cookies with Milk Chocolate Chips, fold 1 cup (170 g) of milk chocolate chips into the batter along with the flour.

Because a version of these cookies won a fab "bake-off" (thank you, Pancake Princess!), it goes without saying that this streamlined rendition is going to be tender, wonderfully peanutty, and chewy—in short, everything anyone could ever want in a PB cookie. The recipe calls for vegetable shortening to help shorten (pun intended) the time between assembly and baking, as it keeps the cookies from spreading as they bake. Without it, the cookies really need a rest in the fridge, which I am against when snackable baking. *However*, do you see those gorgeous cracks in the cookie in the photo? Those (miraculously) appeared post-bake because the dough rested on the counter for a few hours during the *Snackable Bakes* photo shoot. Thus, if sexy, cookbook-worthy-looking PB cookies are your jam, rest away.

1. Heat the oven to 375°F. Line two baking sheets with parchment paper.

2. Whisk the shortening into the butter in a large bowl until the shortening melts (if there are still a few little solid bits of shortening, don't worry). Whisk in the brown sugar and vanilla, and then the eggs, one at a time, and, finally, the peanut butter. Sprinkle the baking soda, baking powder, and kosher salt into the bowl, one at a time, vigorously whisking after each. Gently fold in the flour with a flexible spatula, just until the last streak disappears.

3. Pour the granulated sugar into a shallow bowl. Portion the (very soft and sticky) dough using a ¼-cup portion scoop or measuring cup and nudge each ball of dough around in the sugar before placing it on the prepared baking sheets. You should be able to fit about six per sheet. Sprinkle with the flaky sea salt and bake for 14 to 16 minutes, rotating and swapping the placement of the sheets at the halfway point, until the tops are slightly puffed and crinkly and the cookies are just beginning to brown around the edges.

4. Once removed from the oven, gently press each cookie with a spatula to flatten. Repeat with the remaining dough, cooling the sheets before doing so. Let cool to room temperature before eating (or don't . . .). Keep the cookies in an airtight container on the counter for up to 3 days.

Straight-Up Coconut Macaroons

MAKES ABOUT 24 MACAROONS
ACTIVE TIME: 8 MINUTES
BAKE TIME: 17 TO 20 MINUTES

4 cups (320 g) sweetened shredded coconut

1 tablespoon light corn syrup

1 teaspoon kosher salt

½ cup (118 ml) cream of coconut, such as Coco López, or ½ cup (157 g) sweetened condensed milk

1 teaspoon vanilla extract

1 large egg white, at room temperature

VARIATION

For Straight-Up Coconut Macaroons with Chocolate Chips, fold in ¼ cup (43 g) of semisweet chocolate chips, chopped, after you add the egg white.

At Baked, the bakery where I got my (illustrious) start, one of the first recipes a novice like me was permitted to make was macaroons. The recipe was so easy and one-bowl-ish that the powers-that-be were confident I couldn't mess it up. And luckily for me, they were right (I mean, I screwed up plenty of other things in those early days, but the macaroons were just not one of them). My recipe here is also of the idiot-proof variety, resulting in chewy, delicate, and wonderfully moist macaroons. If you are inclined to track down the cream of coconut, it does add a wonderful boost of flavor, and you can use the extra in the (epic) Coconut Tres Leches Snacking Cake (page 150), but sweetened condensed milk will work, too. Substitute the leftover yolk for a whole egg in one of the snacking cakes or use it in the Individual Butterscotch Puddings (page 180).

1. Heat the oven to 375°F. Line a baking sheet with parchment paper.

2. Stir together all the ingredients, except the egg white, in a large bowl, using a flexible spatula. Whisk the egg white in a small bowl for about 30 seconds, until foamy and tripled in volume. Gently fold the foamy white into the coconut mixture. Portion the macaroons with a 1½-tablespoon portion scoop or measuring spoons, evenly spacing them on the prepared baking sheet. They do not spread. Bake the macaroons for 17 to 20 minutes, rotating them at the halfway point, until they are lightly browned.

3. Remove from the oven and let them cool to room temperature before serving. Keep the macaroons in an airtight container on the counter for up to 3 days.

Tahini Milk Chocolate Bars

MAKES 16 BARS

ACTIVE TIME: 20 MINUTES

BAKE TIME: 20 TO 25 MINUTES

Cooking spray or softened
  unsalted butter for pan

FOR THE BASE

½ cup (113 g) unsalted butter

½ cup (120 g) tahini, well stirred

½ cup (100 g) granulated sugar

¼ cup (80 g) light corn syrup

2¼ cups (222 g) quick 1-minute
  oats

2 teaspoons vanilla extract

¾ teaspoon kosher salt

FOR THE TOPPING

¾ cup (128 g) milk chocolate
  chips

2½ tablespoons tahini, well
  stirred

3 tablespoons heavy cream

1½ tablespoons light corn syrup

Flaky sea salt for sprinkling

These are a take on my MIL's Oh Henry!® bars, a fantastically chewy and flavorful bar cookie, that gives off plenty of the caramel/peanut/chocolate vibes of the actual candy. That is due to a slightly nutty oat base that is briefly cooked on the stovetop, baked, and then topped with a chocolate glaze. They were on regular rotation when my husband was growing up and I'm still jealous about that. Here, I've given them a little tahini makeover (usually they call for peanut butter) and I'm pretty darn excited about it.

1. Heat the oven to 350°F. Grease an 8-inch square cake pan with cooking spray or softened butter. Line the bottom with a long sheet of parchment paper that extends up and over two opposite sides of the pan.

2. To make the base, cook the butter, tahini, sugar, and corn syrup in a medium saucepan over medium heat, stirring occasionally with a flexible spatula, until the mixture just begins to boil. Off the heat, add the oats, vanilla, and kosher salt and stir to combine. Scrape the mixture into the bottom of the prepared pan, creating a solid, even layer, and bake for 20 to 25 minutes, rotating at the halfway point, until the entire surface is bubbling and lightly browned. Remove from the oven and let cool while you make the topping.

3. To make the topping, microwave all the topping ingredients in a small, microwave-safe bowl in two 15-second bursts, stirring after each with a fork, until melted and smooth. Pour the topping over the baked oatmeal base and, using a small offset spatula or the back of a spoon, spread it smoothly and evenly. Refrigerate for at least 2 hours, until the topping is set. Remove the bars from the pan, using the parchment overhang to lift them out. Run a butter knife around the edges if there's resistance. Sprinkle with flaky sea salt, slice into squares, and serve. Keep the bars in an airtight container in the refrigerator for up to 3 days.

Gooey Blondies with Toasty Pecans and Chocolate x 3

MAKES 24 BLONDIES
ACTIVE TIME: 5 MINUTES
BAKE TIME: 23 TO 27 MINUTES

Cooking spray or softened
unsalted butter for pan

1 cup (226 g) unsalted butter,
melted and cooled slightly

2 cups packed (400 g) light
brown sugar

1 tablespoon vanilla extract

2 large eggs

1 teaspoon baking powder

¾ teaspoon kosher salt

1¾ cups (227 g) all-purpose flour

1 cup (112 g) pecans, deeply
toasted and roughly chopped

1 cup (170 g) assorted chocolate
chips, such as dark, milk, and
white

I worship a chewy chocolate chip cookie with crispy edges, soft middles, and pools of molten chocolate as much as the next peep, but I just might love these blondies (basically chocolate chip cookies in bar form) a tiny bit more—and I'm thinking that you might, too. The three different flavors of chocolate, along with the deeply toasted nuts are both key—and if you're by any chance partial to a crackly topped blondie/brownie situation, you're going to be very happy. I give a range of baking times for these, so, if you're into extra-gooey, slightly underbaked blondies (particularly the middle pieces), the lower range is for you. If not, go with the higher one.

1. Heat the oven to 350°F. Grease a 9-by-13-inch pan with cooking spray or softened butter. Line it with a long sheet of parchment paper that extends up and over the two long sides of the pan.

2. Whisk together the butter, brown sugar, and vanilla in a large bowl for 30 seconds. Whisk in the eggs, one at a time. Sprinkle the baking powder and salt into the bowl, one at a time, vigorously whisking after each. Gently fold in the flour just until a few streaks remain. Fold in the pecans and chocolate. Don't overmix. Scrape the batter into the prepared pan and smooth the top.

3. Bake for 23 to 27 minutes, until the top is lightly browned and crackly, the edges are starting to pull away from the sides of the pan, and a wooden skewer inserted into the center comes out with wet crumbs (blondies overbake really easily, hence the wet crumbs . . .).

4. Remove from the oven and let cool in the pan until room temperature, or until just cool enough for the blondies to keep their shape if you want to eat them gooey and melty. Lift the blondies out of the pan by the parchment paper overhang and slice. Keep the blondies in an airtight container on the counter for up to 3 days, although they are *excellent* frozen (place in a resealable plastic bag for up to a month)—I mean, can you say "ice cream sandwich?"

Nutty Oats and Jam "Rebel" Bars

MAKES 16 BARS
ACTIVE TIME: 10 MINUTES
BAKING TIME: 40 MINUTES

Cooking spray or softened
   unsalted butter for pan
1½ cups (140 g) old-fashioned
   oats
1 cup (130 g) all-purpose flour
¾ cup (77 g) walnuts, deeply
   toasted and finely chopped
1 teaspoon kosher salt
½ teaspoon baking soda
½ cup (113 g) unsalted butter,
   melted and cooled slightly
¾ cup (150 g) light brown sugar
1½ teaspoons vanilla extract
1 large egg
1 cup (287 g) of your favorite jam

VARIATION

For Nutty Oats and Chocolate
"Rebel" Bars, replace the jam
with 1 cup (170 g) of semisweet
chocolate chips, melted, combined with half of a 7-ounce
can (198 g) of sweetened condensed milk and ½ teaspoon
of kosher salt. Bake for 32 to
37 minutes. Sprinkle with a little flaky sea salt postbake.

Have you ever heard of a revel bar? Well, I hadn't either, until a few years back when *Cook's Country* featured a recipe for them. They're basically a chocolate-filled oat bar that's a little more cakey than crispy, and a bit more substantial than your average oatmeal jam situation—and they're a no-brainer to assemble, since the base and topping are made from the same dough. Here, I'm being a tad *rebel*lious (hence the name!) and marrying the revel and the oat/fruit sitch by filling my "rebel" bars with jam. The result is a wonderfully addictive, soft, oaty, jammy bar cookie, with a generous, big-crumbed topping. And, yes, chocolate lovers, I included a chocolate variation for you, too, because you are my peeps and I've always got your back.

1. Heat the oven to 350°F. Grease an 8-inch square cake pan with cooking spray or softened butter. Line with a large sheet of parchment paper that extends over two opposite sides of the pan.

2. Whisk together the oats, flour, walnuts, salt, and baking soda in a medium bowl. Whisk together the melted butter, brown sugar, and vanilla in a large bowl for 30 seconds, then whisk in the egg. Gently fold the dry ingredients into the wet with a flexible spatula just until the last streak of oats/flour disappears. Scrape half of the dough into the prepared pan and press it flat; it'll be sticky. Spread with jam and top with the remaining (sticky) dough, portioning it into bits with your fingers and scattering it evenly to cover.

3. Bake for about 40 minutes, or until the topping is nicely browned. Remove from the oven and let cool in the pan to room temperature, about 2 hours, and then run a butter knife around the edges and lift the bars out of the pan by the parchment overhang, before slicing into squares and serving. Keep the rebels in an airtight container in the refrigerator for up to 3 days.

Coconut Loaf Cake with Coconut Glaze

MAKES ONE 8½-BY-4½-INCH
LOAF CAKE
ACTIVE TIME: 15 MINUTES
BAKE TIME: 60 TO 65 MINUTES

Cooking spray or softened
  unsalted butter for pan

FOR THE CAKE

¾ cup (177 ml) coconut oil, melted
  if solid, or vegetable oil

1⅓ cups (267 g) granulated sugar

1½ teaspoons coconut extract
  (optional, but encouraged)

¼ teaspoon vanilla extract

3 large eggs, at room
  temperature

¾ cup (177 ml) very cold tap
  water, or full-fat coconut milk

2 teaspoons baking powder

¾ teaspoon kosher salt

2 cups (260 g) all-purpose flour

1⅓ cups (107 g) sweetened shredded coconut, plus 2 *toasted*
  tablespoons for sprinkling

FOR THE GLAZE

1 cup (120 g) confectioners' sugar

4 teaspoons tap water, at room
  temperature, or full-fat coconut milk

½ teaspoon coconut extract or
  vanilla extract

If you are even *remotely* team coconut, you need to make this cake. It has the most delightfully moist and shaggy crumb, almost like a macaroon, and the coconut flavor really shines due to a little coconut extract both in the cake and glaze (but leave it out if you're anti-extracts other than vanilla—and substitute an additional ¾ teaspoon of vanilla in its place). The recipe also calls for some cold water, which is a little weird, I know, but it actually contributes to the cake's special texture (just please don't ask me how). However, if you're feeling fancy, you can substitute full-fat coconut milk (both in the cake and glaze) for the water.

1. Heat the oven to 350°F. Grease an 8½-by-4½-inch loaf pan with cooking spray or softened butter. Line the bottom with a long sheet of parchment paper that extends up and over the long sides of the pan (like a cradle for your cake).

2. To make the cake, whisk together the oil, granulated sugar, and extracts in a large bowl for 30 seconds. Whisk in the eggs, one at a time, and then the cold water. Sprinkle the baking powder and the salt into the bowl, one at a time, vigorously whisking after each. Gently fold in the flour with a flexible spatula just until a few streaks remain. Fold in 1⅓ cups (107 g) of the sweetened shredded coconut. Transfer the batter to the prepared pan, smooth the top, and bake for 60 to 65 minutes, rotating at the halfway point. The cake is done when a wooden skewer inserted into the center comes out with a moist crumb or two.

3. Remove from the oven and let cool in the pan for about 20 minutes, or until you can safely lift the cake out by the parchment overhang without burning yourself. Run a butter knife around the edges if it resists. Let cool to room temperature while you make the glaze.

4. To make the glaze, whisk together the confectioners' sugar, water, and your choice of extract in a small bowl until thick yet pourable, adding more water or more sugar as necessary. Decoratively pour the glaze over the cake and sprinkle with the 2 tablespoons of toasted shredded coconut. Let the glaze set, about 15 minutes, before slicing and serving. Keep the cake, wrapped, on the counter for up to 3 days.

Farm Dinner Zucchini Loaf with Walnuts

MAKES ONE 8½-BY-4½-INCH
LOAF CAKE
ACTIVE TIME: 10 MINUTES
BAKE TIME: 60 TO 70 MINUTES

Cooking spray or softened
  unsalted butter for pan

2 cups (260 g) all-purpose flour

1¼ teaspoons baking soda

1½ teaspoons ground cinnamon

1 teaspoon kosher salt

⅔ cup (158 ml) vegetable oil

1⅓ cups packed (266 g) light
  brown sugar

1¼ teaspoons vanilla extract

2 large eggs, at room
  temperature

2⅔ cups (273 g) shredded,
  unpeeled zucchini (using the
  large holes of a box grater)

1⅓ cups (120 g) walnuts, toasted
  and chopped into small(ish)
  pieces

VARIATION

For Double Chocolate Farm
Dinner Zucchini Loaf with
Walnuts, substitute ¾ cup
(60 g) of Dutch-processed
cocoa powder for ¾ cup (97 g)
of the all-purpose flour and
add 1 cup (170 g) of semisweet
chocolate chips when you
add the zucchini and nuts.
Bake for 70 to 80 minutes.
Serve with dollops of Cream
Cheese Whipped Cream
(page 52); omitting the kirsch
and preserves.

My love of zucchini bread goes back to my bakery days, as the loaf at Baked was so moist (due to the zucchini), vegetal (in a good way), nutty (due to pecans), and just perfectly sweetened. My snackable version here is an ode to that, studded with deeply toasted walnuts, that is even better on day two—particularly when generously spread with cream cheese (when you know, you know). Years ago, I developed a chocolate version of this loaf (because chocolate and zucchini are BFFs) to serve at a farm dinner in Far Rockaway, New York, and if that sounds yum to you, the variation is below.

1. Heat the oven to 350°F. Grease an 8½-by-4½-inch loaf pan with cooking spray or softened butter. Line the bottom with a long sheet of parchment paper that extends up and over the two long sides of the pan (like a cradle for your loaf).

2. Whisk together the flour, baking soda, cinnamon, and salt in a medium bowl. Whisk together the oil, brown sugar, and vanilla in a large bowl for 30 seconds, then whisk in the eggs, one at a time. Gently fold the dry ingredients into the wet with a flexible spatula just until a few streaks of flour remain. Fold in the zucchini and nuts. Transfer the batter to the prepared pan, smooth the top, and bake for 60 to 70 minutes, rotating at the halfway point. The loaf is done when a wooden skewer inserted into the center comes out with only a moist crumb or two.

3. Remove from the oven and let cool in the pan for about 20 minutes, or until you can safely lift the loaf out by the parchment overhang without burning yourself. Run a butter knife around the edges if it resists. Let cool to room temperature before slicing and serving. Keep the loaf, wrapped, on the counter for up to 3 days.

Hazelnut Chip Snacking Cake with Chocolate Hazelnut Whipped Cream

MAKES ONE 8-INCH SQUARE CAKE

ACTIVE TIME: 20 MINUTES

BAKE TIME: 35 TO 40 MINUTES

Cooking spray or softened unsalted butter for pan

FOR THE CAKE

½ cup (54 g) hazelnut flour

¾ cup (107 g) skinless hazelnuts, chopped finely

1 cup (130 g) all-purpose flour

1½ teaspoons baking powder

½ teaspoon kosher salt

6 ounces (170 g) semisweet chocolate, chopped, or 1 cup (170 g) semisweet chocolate chips, chopped

½ cup (113 g) unsalted butter, melted and cooled slightly

1 cup packed (200 g) light brown sugar

1 teaspoon vanilla extract

2 large eggs

¾ cup (173 g) sour cream

FOR THE WHIPPED CREAM

1 cup (237 ml) heavy cream

⅓ cup (100 g) chocolate hazelnut spread, such as Nutella®

Hazelnut and chocolate is a match made in heaven and this super-moist, chocolate-studded cake with a "nutty" vibe due to (toasted!) hazelnut flour and nuts, and an otherworldly chocolate hazelnut whipped cream (made with a chocolate hazelnut spread, such as everybody's fave, Nutella®) showcases that match like nobody's business. Toasting the nuts and flour really pops the hazelnut flavor, but I get it if toasting flour seems fussy and you want to skip it. To make your own hazelnut flour, see page 14; and, if you cannot find skinless nuts, see page 119 for instructions on how to remove the skins. And I like bar chocolate here, off-brand (I know), so you get lots of chocolate splinters and fine pieces throughout the cake, but you can also just chop chips.

1. Heat the oven to 350°F. Grease an 8-inch square cake pan with cooking spray or softened butter. Line with a long piece of parchment paper that extends up and over two opposite edges of the pan.

2. To make the cake, spread the hazelnut flour on half of a baking sheet and the chopped hazelnuts on the other half—you want to keep them separate—and toast for about 10 minutes, stirring the flour at the halfway point. Let cool before proceeding.

3. Whisk together the cooled hazelnut flour, ½ cup (67 g) of the toasted nuts, and the all-purpose flour, baking powder, and salt in a medium bowl. Whisk in the chopped chocolate. Whisk together the butter, brown sugar, and vanilla in a large bowl for 30 seconds; whisk in the eggs, one at a time, and then the sour cream. Gently fold in the dry ingredients with a flexible spatula just until the last streak disappears. Don't overmix.

4. Scrape the batter into the prepared pan and bake for 35 to 40 minutes, rotating the pan at the halfway point, until a wooden skewer inserted into the center comes out with a moist crumb or two. Remove from the oven and let cool in the pan for about 20 minutes, or until you can safely lift the cake out by the parchment overhang without burning yourself. Run a butter knife around the edges if it resists. Let cool to room temperature before topping with the whipped cream.

5. To make the whipped cream, whisk the cream on medium to medium-high speed in the bowl of a stand mixer fitted with the whisk attachment until medium peaks form. Reduce the speed to medium and add the chocolate hazelnut spread, a couple of tablespoons at a time. Once all of it has been added, remove the bowl from the mixer and finish folding it in by hand with a flexible spatula. Decoratively top the cake with the whipped cream, making lots of swoops and swirls with the back of a spoon. Sprinkle with the remaining toasted hazelnuts, cut into slices, and serve. The cake is best the day it is made (due to the frosting) but will keep, wrapped, in the refrigerator for up to 3 days.

Almond Olive Oil Snacking Cake with Chocolate Almond Glaze

MAKES ONE 8-INCH ROUND CAKE
ACTIVE TIME: 15 MINUTES
BAKE TIME: 33 TO 38 MINUTES

Cooking spray, softened
  unsalted butter, or olive oil
  for pan

FOR THE CAKE
1¼ cups (163 g) all-purpose flour
¼ cup plus 2 tablespoons (38 g)
  almond flour
1½ teaspoons baking powder
½ teaspoon kosher salt
1 cup (200 g) granulated sugar
½ cup (118 ml) extra-virgin olive oil
¾ teaspoon almond extract
½ teaspoon vanilla extract
2 large eggs
¾ cup (177 ml) almond milk or
  whole cow's milk

FOR THE GLAZE
¾ cup (127 g) semisweet chocolate chips (vegan, if desired)
3 tablespoons almond milk or
  whole cow's milk

¼ cup (30 g) blanched, sliced
  almonds, toasted, for
  decorating

If prepared with almond milk and vegan chocolate chips, this cake is a dairy-free wonder, on the off chance you are into that sort of thing. Moreover, the cake is divine, with the softest and most plush crumb in all the (snackable bakes) land. And the combo of almond, olive oil, and chocolate is just a win-win. The cake calls for almond extract, so if a grocery store run needs to happen in order to make this little number, word to the wise: stock up. The cake is so good, there's no way you will make it only once—and you'll also need almond extract for the Pistachio Chocolate Anytime Buns (page 116), which I am certain you've already placed on your need-to-bake list.

1. Heat the oven to 350°F. Grease an 8-inch round cake pan with cooking spray or softened butter (or brush with olive oil, to keep it nondairy). Line the bottom with parchment paper.

2. To make the cake, whisk together the flours, baking powder, and salt in a medium bowl. Whisk together the sugar, oil, and extracts in a large bowl for 30 seconds; whisk in the eggs, one at a time, and then the almond milk. Gently fold in the dry ingredients with a flexible spatula just until the last streak disappears. Scrape the batter into the prepared pan and bake for 33 to 38 minutes, rotating at the halfway point, until a wooden skewer inserted into the center comes out with a moist crumb or two.

3. Remove from the oven and let cool 10 to 15 minutes, then invert the cake onto a cooling rack, right side up, running a knife around the edges if it resists. Let cool to room temperature before glazing.

4. To make the glaze, microwave the chocolate and almond milk together in a microwave-safe bowl on HIGH in 30-second bursts, stirring with a fork after each, until the chocolate melts. Pour the glaze over the cake and sprinkle with the almonds before serving. Keep the cake, wrapped, on the counter for up to 3 days.

Dreamiest Peanut Butter Chocolate Cup

MAKES ONE 9½-INCH TART
ACTIVE TIME: 10 MINUTES
INACTIVE TIME: 1 HOUR

3 cups (510 g) milk chocolate chips

3 tablespoons vegetable oil

1½ cups (375 g) smooth peanut butter, not all-natural

1⅔ cups (200 g) confectioners' sugar

6 tablespoons (85 g) unsalted butter, melted and cooled slightly

1 teaspoon vanilla extract

1 teaspoon kosher salt

Okay, so most importantly, this is a magnificent snackable treat to make for all the Reese's Peanut Butter Cup lovers in your life (and if you're doing life right, there should be many). It *does* require a 9½-inch tart pan with a removable bottom (and preferably fluted edges, for the quintessentially "Reese's" look) and maybe you're mad at me 'cause you don't own one and you don't want to buy one, but I promise it is worth it due to the many (many) times you will be making this (dare I say) iconic confection. In a pinch, a 9½-inch springform pan will work, too.

1. Have ready a 9½-inch tart pan with fluted sides and a removable bottom, as well as a baking sheet.

2. Microwave 1½ cups (255 g) of the chips and 1½ tablespoons of the oil on HIGH in a medium, microwave-safe bowl in 20-second bursts, stirring with a flexible spatula after each one, until smooth, about 40 seconds total. Spread the melted chocolate on the bottom of the tart pan and up the sides (as best you can) with the back of a spoon. Don't wash the bowl, as you'll use it again. Place the tart pan on the baking sheet and put it into the freezer to chill until the chocolate is set, about 15 minutes.

3. Whisk together the peanut butter, confectioners' sugar, butter, vanilla, and salt in a large bowl until smooth. Transfer the peanut butter mixture to the chocolate-coated tart pan and evenly spread with a flexible spatula.

4. Microwave the remaining chocolate and oil in the same microwave-safe bowl you used previously, and pour it over the peanut butter filling, smoothing the top with an offset spatula, if you have one, or your flexible spatula.

5. Freeze for about 45 minutes to an hour, until the sides of the pan easily pop off (the longer you wait, the easier they will pop). Once removed, and using a small paring knife, dislodge the base from the bottom of the cup. Slice with a large chef's knife, dipping the knife in hot water and drying it in between cuts for the cleanest slices. Keep the cup, wrapped, in the refrigerator for up to a week.

Coconut Brigadieros with Chocolate Sprinkles

MAKES 20 CANDIES
ACTIVE TIME: 15 MINUTES
INACTIVE TIME: 30 TO 45 MINUTES

Cooking spray or softened unsalted butter for plate

1 cup (290 g) sweetened condensed milk

¾ cup (62 g) unsweetened grated coconut

⅓ cup (79 ml) heavy cream

1 tablespoon unsalted butter

1 teaspoon light corn syrup

½ teaspoon vanilla extract

½ teaspoon kosher salt

Chocolate sprinkles for rolling

Who knew that one of my OG favorites (sweetened condensed milk) was the main attraction in brigadieros, a traditional Brazilian (easy-peasy) candy that I was originally introduced to by my friend Anna in her book, *Heirloom Kitchen*. These darlings are chewy and sweet and the coconut marries perfectly with the chocolate sprinkles, giving them all the best Mounds bar feels. The leftover condensed milk should be used ASAP to make a batch of Secret Ingredient Crispy Rice Cereal Treats (page 73), and you can substitute coconut milk for the heavy cream and roll all the candies in grated coconut, rather than the sprinkles if you're feeling extra coconutty.

1. Grease a dinner plate with cooking spray or softened butter.

2. Heat the sweetened condensed milk, ½ cup (41 g) of the coconut, heavy cream, butter, and corn syrup together in a medium pot over medium-high heat, stirring constantly with a flexible spatula, until the mixture begins to bubble. Lower the heat a little, to medium(ish), and continue to cook, stirring, until the mixture thickens and when you scrape your spatula along the bottom of the pot, it leaves a trail that lasts for a few seconds. This will take about 10 minutes. If your mixture is not bubbling at all once you lower the heat, you can nudge the heat up a bit, or, alternatively, if it looks like the bottom is scorching, bring it down.

3. Off the heat, add the vanilla and salt and stir to combine. Pour the mixture onto the prepared plate. Freeze for 30 to 45 minutes, until quite firm, but not frozen.

4. Pour the chocolate sprinkles and remaining ¼ cup (21 g) of the coconut into two separate small, shallow bowls. Roll the mixture into 1-inch balls, about a tablespoon each, and then roll half of the balls in the sprinkles and the other half in the coconut. Serve immediately or refrigerate them briefly. They're extra-fudgy when chilled. Keep the brigadieros in an airtight container on the counter or in the refrigerator for up to 3 days.

Sparkle Plenty Peanut Butter Marshmallow Fudge

MAKES 36 LARGE PIECES
OR 64 TINY ONES
ACTIVE TIME: 8 MINUTES
SET-UP TIME: 2 HOURS

Cooking spray or softened
   unsalted butter for pan
16 ounces (453 g) peanut butter
   chips
¼ cup (65 g) smooth peanut butter, not all-natural
One 14-ounce can (397 g) sweetened condensed milk
1 tablespoon vanilla extract
1½ teaspoons kosher salt
3 cups (135 g) mini marshmallows
1½ cups (200 g) salted and
   roasted peanuts, coarsely
   chopped
Flaky sea salt for sprinkling
Turbinado sugar for sprinkling

What can I say? This delicious, peanut-forward fudge will remind you of your favorite (or what *should* have been your favorite) childhood sandwich (the fluffernutter), and it is made entirely in your microwave (if that's how you roll), and takes no time to assemble—in other words, it is the ideal confection. In fact, it is so full of flavorful pizzazz and is so delectably sparkly that I coined it "sparkle plenty," a name I was affectionately called as a towheaded little girl, by a beloved family friend.

1. Grease an 8-inch square cake pan with cooking spray or softened butter. Line with a long sheet of parchment paper that extends up and over two opposite sides of the pan.

2. Microwave the peanut butter chips, peanut butter, and sweetened condensed milk together on HIGH in a large, microwave-safe bowl in two 45-second bursts, stirring after each with a flexible spatula, until the chips and peanut butter are melted. Once melted and stirred, the texture will change to something more fudgy and thick: don't be alarmed.

3. Stir in the vanilla and kosher salt, and then the marshmallows and nuts. Scrape the fudge into the prepared pan. Drape with a sheet of parchment paper and flatten with your hands. Sprinkle with flaky sea salt and turbinado sugar.

4. Refrigerate until firm, about 2 hours, then slice with a chef's knife. Keep the fudge in an airtight container on the counter for up to a week.

Kathy's Sugar and Spice Pecans

MAKES 1 POUND OF NUTS
ACTIVE TIME: 5 MINUTES
BAKE TIME: 1 HOUR

1 large egg white
1 tablespoon water
1 teaspoon vanilla extract
1 pound (455 g) pecans
1 cup (200 g) granulated sugar
1½ teaspoons kosher salt
1 teaspoon ground cinnamon
½ teaspoon freshly grated nutmeg
⅛ teaspoon cayenne pepper, or up to ¼ teaspoon, if you like things "zippy"

Kathy is a pal o' mine who I have actually never met IRL. She lives in Wisconsin and first contacted me when I was on a book tour, for my second book, *The Vintage Baker*. She had read about me and my love of old-fashioned recipes in her local paper and wanted to share some from her collection. I loved her for that, and, in fact have never stopped loving her, as she has never stopped sharing. We are in touch on the regular, whenever she stumbles upon something in her trove that she thinks I might like, and I could not be more grateful to her (or to these pecans—which are sweet and salty and spicy and just plain fantabulous). Wondering about what to do with the leftover yolk? Save it for the Individual Butterscotch Puddings (page 180), or substitute it for one of the whole eggs in a snacking cake for a little extra moisture.

1. Heat the oven to 250°F. Line a baking sheet with parchment paper.

2. Whisk together the egg white, water, and vanilla in a medium bowl until frothy. Add the pecans and stir with a flexible spatula until well coated. Whisk together the sugar, salt, cinnamon, nutmeg, and cayenne in a large bowl. Pour in the pecans and stir to coat. Evenly spread the nuts onto the prepared baking sheet and bake for 1 hour, tossing every 15 minutes. Remove from the oven and let the nuts cool to room temperature on the baking sheet before serving. Keep the pecans in an airtight container for up to a month.

CHAPTER 5. # Dairy Delights

Oh, gosh: talk about a favorite chapter. I mean, not only do all of these sublime, creamy recipes include whipped cream as a component (and whipped cream is one of life's most light and fluffy pleasures, in case you did not know), but they are also all of the *make-ahead* variety, meaning they are perfect for any and all entertaining. And if you're anything like me, entertaining is ONLY fun IF, once your guests arrive, you have already finished all your cooking and sweets-making, so you can chat and chomp (and maybe drink) with abandon. There should be no looking at timers and running into the kitchen to pull a pie or cake or crumble from the oven (one that you've undoubtedly already burned due to the abovementioned chomping, etc.). One of my favorite treats to prepare in advance is an icebox cake, and I am a lover of said cakes from way back (my first book is basically a love letter to them), as all they (really) require is the ability to layer store-bought cookies with cream. Hoping you will grow to appreciate them, too (if you don't already), as well as some of my other cherished dairy-forward, make-ahead items, such as no-churn ice cream (so simple and luxuriously creamy) and bread pudding, which falls somewhere between a cake and a pudding—and is my forever love. My older son, Oliver, feels about tiramisu the way I feel about all of the above, and tres leches, too, is a make-ahead dairy-delight of the finest caliber, particularly when coconut flavored. So, I think you get it: these recipes are all absolute must-makes in my book (both literally and figuratively).

Coconut Tres Leches Snacking Cake

MAKES ONE 8-INCH SQUARE CAKE

ACTIVE TIME: 20 MINUTES

BAKE TIME: 23 TO 27 MINUTES

Cooking spray or softened unsalted butter for pan

FOR THE CAKE

1 cup (200 g) granulated sugar

½ cup (118 ml) coconut oil, melted, or vegetable oil

2 teaspoons coconut extract (optional, but encouraged)

½ teaspoon vanilla extract

2 large eggs

¼ cup (59 ml) full-fat canned coconut milk

1½ teaspoons baking powder

½ teaspoon kosher salt

1½ cups (195 g) all-purpose flour

FOR THE MILKY SOAK

1 cup (237 ml) cream of coconut, such as Coco López, well stirred, or 1 cup (237 ml) sweetened condensed milk plus ¾ teaspoon coconut extract, or to taste

¾ cup (177 ml) evaporated milk

¼ cup (59 ml) full-fat canned coconut milk

FOR THE WHIPPED CREAM

1½ cups (355 ml) heavy cream

2 tablespoons confectioners' sugar

⅓ cup (18 g) unsweetened coconut flakes, toasted, for decorating (optional)

A tres leches cake is a relatively easy cake, but here I've made it more than easy, I've made it snackable. Rather than call for the traditional sponge (requiring the separating of eggs, etc.), all you do here is make a simple one-bowl coconut cake and call it a day. A little poking, pouring, and whipping, and it's snack time.

1. Heat the oven to 350°F. Grease an 8-inch square cake pan with cooking spray or softened butter.

2. To make the cake, whisk together the granulated sugar, oil, coconut extract (if using), and vanilla in a medium bowl for 30 seconds. Whisk in the eggs and the coconut milk. Sprinkle the baking powder and salt into the bowl, one at a time, vigorously whisking after each. Gently fold in the flour just until the last streak disappears. Scrape the batter into the prepared pan (it will be thick) and bake for 23 to 27 minutes, rotating at the halfway point. The cake is ready when a wooden skewer inserted into the center comes out clean and the cake has begun to come away from the sides of the pan (you want the cake to be *very slightly* on the dryer side of perfectly baked). Remove from the oven and let cool.

3. To make the milky soak, whisk together all its ingredients in a 2-cup glass measuring cup. Poke the warm cake with a fork or wooden skewer all over its surface, making lots of deep holes that extend to the bottom of the pan. Run a butter knife around the edges of the cake to release them from the pan, then slowly pour 1½ cups (355 ml) of the milk mixture over the cake, pausing to let the liquid soak in as you do so. Wait for five minutes and then pour the final ½ cup (118 ml) of soak over the cake, concentrating on the edges, where it will pool a bit. Refrigerate for at least 2 hours, uncovered—the cake may not have absorbed all the milk at this point, but it will still be scrumptious—or overnight. If chilling overnight, cover the pan in plastic wrap once cool.

4. To make the whipped cream, whisk together the cream and confectioners' sugar on medium to medium-high speed in the bowl of a stand mixer fitted with the whisk attachment, until soft peaks form. Spread the cream over the cake, sprinkle the toasted coconut on top (if using), slice, and serve. Keep the cake, covered, in the refrigerator for up to 3 days.

VARIATION

For Traditional Tres Leches Cake, substitute vegetable oil for the coconut oil, omit the coconut extract and increase the vanilla to 1½ teaspoons, and substitute whole milk for the full-fat canned coconut milk in the cake. For the milky soak, substitute sweetened condensed milk for the cream of coconut, and whole milk for the full-fat canned coconut milk. Omit the toasted coconut flakes.

Salted Honey Ginger Icebox Cake

MAKES ONE 8½-BY-4½-INCH
LOAF CAKE
ACTIVE TIME: 10 MINUTES
INACTIVE TIME: 6 TO 8 HOURS

2 cups (474 ml) heavy cream
½ cup (160 g) honey, plus more
    for drizzling
¾ teaspoon kosher salt, or to
    taste
About 25 crispy, 2-inch ginger-
    snap cookies (160 g), such as
    Nabisco brand, plus one or
    two more for crumbling and
    decorating
Flaky sea salt for sprinkling

I'm a self-proclaimed salt-aholic and, for me, this cake is all about the way the salt plays with the honey. Honestly, I'm not even like a huge honey fan (sorry, honey lovers). But gosh, when you fold it into a slightly salty whipped cream and layer it with gingersnaps? It will completely wow you, as it has me. So good and yet so simple.

1. Line an 8½-by-4½-inch loaf pan with two long pieces of plastic wrap that overhang both the sides and ends of the pan (the plastic should be long enough so that once you have filled the pan, you can stretch it over the top to cover the cake).

2. Whisk together the cream, honey, and kosher salt on medium to medium-high speed in the bowl of a stand mixer fitted with the whisk attachment, until medium to stiff peaks form. Fill the prepared pan with half of the whipped cream. Position the pan so one of the short ends is nearest you and begin wedging upright cookies in horizontal rows of six (like dominoes) starting at the short end nearest you and continuing until you reach the other short end. Top with the rest of the whipped cream and cover the cake with the plastic wrap overhang. Place in the refrigerator to chill for 6 to 8 hours, or overnight.

3. Invert the cake onto a serving plate, remove the pan, and peel off the plastic. Crush a few gingersnaps in a mortar and pestle (if you have one) or in a resealable plastic bag with a rolling pin (if you do not), and sprinkle the crumbs over the top of the cake, along with a drizzle of honey and a few flakes of sea salt. Slice the cake with a large chef's knife, dipping the knife in hot water and drying it in between cuts for the cleanest slices. Serve slices with additional honey and flaky sea salt. Keep the cake, wrapped, in the refrigerator for up to 3 days.

S'more Icebox Cake

MAKES ONE 8½-BY-4½-INCH
LOAF CAKE

ACTIVE TIME: 15 MINUTES

INACTIVE TIME: 6 TO 8 HOURS

FOR THE GANACHE

1 cup (170 g) semisweet chocolate chips

½ cup (118 ml) heavy cream

¼ teaspoon kosher salt

FOR THE WHIPPED CREAM

2 cups (474 ml) heavy cream

2 teaspoons vanilla extract

¼ teaspoon kosher salt

One 7-ounce jar (198 g) marshmallow crème

About 9 full graham crackers (144 g), one sleeve, plus more for decorating

I mean, "s'more icebox cake." Need I say (s')more? Simple, delicious, and easy on the eye: the most difficult thing about this cake is the fact that you have to wait a few hours for it to set up in the refrigerator before you can indulge. Delayed gratification is *always* hard, and I won't lie—it's extra hard here.

1. To make the ganache, microwave the chips, heavy cream, and salt together in a medium, microwave-safe bowl on HIGH in 30-second bursts, stirring after each, until melted. Let the ganache cool to room temperature.

2. Line an 8½-by-4½-inch loaf pan with two long pieces of plastic wrap that generously overhang all sides of the pan.

3. To make the whipped cream, whisk together the heavy cream, vanilla, and salt on medium to medium-high speed in the bowl of a stand mixer fitted with the whisk attachment, until medium to stiff peaks form. Whisk in the marshmallow crème on medium-low speed. Spread 1 cup (237 ml) of cream on the bottom of the prepared pan. Spread a layer of ganache on a cracker and place it on the cream, *chocolate side down.* Repeat with more crackers, about 2¼ full crackers per layer, breaking them as necessary, until you have covered the cream in chocolate-covered crackers. Continue to layer in this fashion until you reach the top of the pan or run out. If you have leftover ganache, save it for drizzling over the cake before serving. Cover the top of the cake with the plastic wrap overhang. Place in the refrigerator to chill for 6 to 8 hours, or overnight.

4. Invert the cake onto a serving plate, remove the pan, and peel off the plastic. Crush a graham cracker in a mortar and pestle or in a resealable plastic bag with a rolling pin, and sprinkle the crumbs on top of the cake. Drizzle with any leftover ganache warmed in the microwave and slice the cake with a large chef's knife, dipping the knife in hot water, and drying it, in between cuts for the cleanest slices. Keep the cake, wrapped, in the refrigerator for up to 3 days.

Lemon Pucker Shortbread Icebox Cake

MAKES ONE 8-INCH ROUND CAKE
ACTIVE TIME: 10 MINUTES
INACTIVE TIME: 6 TO 8 HOURS

3 cups (711 g) heavy cream

1¼ teaspoons lemon extract

1 cup (120 g) confectioners' sugar

3 tablespoons lemon zest

¼ cup plus 2 tablespoons (88 ml) freshly squeezed lemon juice

One 10-ounce box thin, crispy shortbread cookies, such as Lorna Doones®

Yellow sparkling sugar for sprinkling

Pucker up, peeps: this one is bracingly lemony (in all the best and most refreshing ways). But a couple of words to the lemon-pucker wise: don't forget to zest your lemons *before* juicing them. During its rest in the fridge, the (perfectly sweet/tart) lemon cream here thickens a little differently than in other icebox cakes, due to the combo of citrus and dairy—no biggie, but just thought you should know. Share this sunshiny cake with the lemon lovers in your life, as this cake is for them.

1. Line an 8-inch round cake pan with two long pieces of plastic wrap that overhang and completely cover the sides of the pan (the plastic should be long enough so that once you have filled the pan, you can stretch it over the top to cover the cake).

2. Whisk the cream, lemon extract, and confectioners' sugar on medium to medium-high speed in the bowl of a stand mixer fitted with the whisk attachment, until soft peaks form. Whisk in the zest and juice until medium to stiff peaks form. Spread one-third of the cream on the bottom of the prepared pan. Top with about 20 cookies and repeat with another layer of cream and another layer of cookies (you may have a few cookies left over—lucky you). Top with a final layer of whipped cream (it may reach above the edge of the pan by a little—no worries) and cover the cake with the plastic wrap overhang. Place in the refrigerator to chill for 6 to 8 hours, or overnight.

3. Invert the cake onto a serving plate, remove the pan, and peel off the plastic. Run an offset spatula or butter knife, dipped in hot water and dried, along the sides to smooth, if you so desire, and sprinkle the sparkling sugar over the top of the cake. Slice the cake with a large chef's knife, dipping the knife in hot water and drying it in between cuts for the cleanest slices. Keep the cake, wrapped, in the refrigerator for up to 3 days.

Blue Ribbon Chocolate Chip Bread Pudding

MAKES ABOUT 9 SERVINGS
ACTIVE TIME: 5 MINUTES
BAKE TIME: ABOUT 40 MINUTES

Cooking spray or softened
   unsalted butter for pan

4 large eggs

2½ cups (592 ml) heavy cream (if
   you are feeling extra) or whole
   milk (if you are not), plus more
   cream for drizzling

½ cup (100 g) granulated sugar

1 teaspoon vanilla extract

¾ teaspoon ground cinnamon

½ teaspoon kosher salt

½ pound (227 g) brioche or challah, preferably stale, cut into
   ½-inch cubes

¾ cup (127 g) semisweet chocolate chips

Turbinado sugar for sprinkling

This is a "blue ribbon" bread pudding not only because it is excellent and therefore deserves a ribbon at the county fair (although I'm not sure that there are bread pudding contests at fairs, but whatevs), but also because I was first introduced to chocolate chip bread pudding *at* Blue Ribbon, a favorite restaurant of mine from (way) back in the day. I am a big fan of bread pudding (which is not surprising, as I am also a lover of French toast) and there is something about egg-soaked bread (whether baked or fried) that just agrees with me. The sprinkle of chips here pays homage to Blue Ribbon's pud, but is optional, if you'd prefer yours sans chips. Prepping the pudding takes less than 5 minutes and results in a fantastic make-ahead treat: just wrap tightly in plastic wrap after assembling, refrigerate overnight, and be sure to add a few minutes to the bake time the next day.

1. Heat the oven to 375°F. Grease a 1½- to 2-quart baking dish with cooking spray or softened butter.

2. Whisk together the eggs, cream, granulated sugar, vanilla, cinnamon, and salt in a large bowl. Add the cubed bread and toss with your hands, or fold with a flexible spatula, to coat. Toss/fold in the chips. Transfer just the bread and chips, not the liquid, to the prepared pan first, using your hands or a slotted spoon. Then, pour the remaining egg mixture from the bowl over the bread (if you just scrape it all in at once, your chips will end up on the bottom of the pan).

3. Sprinkle with the turbinado sugar and bake for about 40 minutes, rotating at the halfway point, until lightly browned and slightly puffed, and with an internal temp of around 170°F. Remove from the oven and serve slices warm with a drizzle of heavy cream. Keep the pudding, wrapped, in the refrigerator for up to 3 days.

Sweetened Condensed Milk Is My Baking BFF

My obsessive love of sweetened condensed milk (or, as I affectionately refer to it, SCM) truthfully knows no bounds. It kind of feels like *every single recipe* that calls for SCM ends up being on my top ten list. This is due in part to its inherent tastiness (SCM is a thick, sweetened milk that has had 60 percent of its water removed, thus intensifying its flavor) but also because of the witchcraft it performs in every treat to which it is included. I mean, when you stir it into melted chocolate, you miraculously make (thermometer–less) fudge; when you fold it into whipped cream, you've got ice cream; when you beat it into cream cheese, you've got cheesecake; when you pour it over cake, you've got a tres leches situation—and one that you will be writing home about for years to come; and when you melt it along with the marshies and butter in Rice Krispies Treats® (RKTs), I mean, well, you've basically made my favorite thing ever. SCM is literally a wonder-ingredient in light of its transformative dessert powers—and is thus always found in this snackable baker's pantry. I mean, if a single ingredient can literally morph other ingredients into some of the most wonderful, easiest-peasiest treats around, and without being showy or in your face (note well: the vast majority of the sweets lovers in your life will have no idea why your RKTs are so spectacular or how you made ice cream without a machine or a cheesecake without an oven), then all I can say is SCM for life, and all that. And I'm pretty sure you might end up feeling the same once you've given a few of the treats that call for it herein a go.

Peppermint Stick No-Churn Ice Cream Sundaes

MAKES 1½ QUARTS OF ICE CREAM
ACTIVE TIME: 5 MINUTES
INACTIVE TIME: 4 TO 6 HOURS

One 14-ounce can (397 g) sweetened condensed milk

1 teaspoon peppermint extract

½ teaspoon vanilla extract

½ teaspoon kosher salt

2 cups (474 ml) heavy cream, cold

1 to 2 drops red food coloring (optional, but encouraged)

½ cup (90 g) finely crushed candy canes or peppermint candies, such as starlight mints

Dad's Hot Fudge Sauce (page 233) for serving

Extremely Special Whipped cream (page 230) for serving

Oh, gosh, do I love peppermint stick ice cream: a love born of childhood trips with my dad to Brigham's, an ice cream parlor near our home. I always ordered it with hot fudge sauce and whipped cream (and I highly recommend you enjoy it that way, too). Here, a little mint extract and red food coloring, plus crushed candy canes or red starlight mints, transform a ho-hum quart of no-churn ice cream into something super nostalgic, and capable of giving you all the joyful, wide-eyed feels of eating ice cream as a kid at a counter, on a stool that swiveled (or is that just me?). Anyway, I'll spare you the sentimentality, and just say, if you're a fan of mint ice cream, I think you are going to dig peppermint stick. But remember, when crushing your candy, place it in a resealable plastic bag, cover with a tea towel, and smash with a rolling pin—otherwise, you risk showering your kitchen with tiny splinters of sticky mint candy (been there, done that).

1. Place an 8½-by-4½-inch metal loaf pan in the freezer.

2. Whisk together the sweetened condensed milk, the two extracts, and the salt in a large bowl. Whisk together the heavy cream and food coloring, if using, on medium to medium-high speed in the bowl of a stand mixer fitted with the whisk attachment, until stiff peaks form. Gently fold the whipped cream into the milk mixture in two installments, then fold in the crushed candy canes. Scrape the ice cream into the cold pan, smooth the top, and tightly cover in plastic wrap. Freeze for 4 to 6 hours, depending on how soft you like your ice cream (I'm partial to soft here, in case you were wondering). If frozen solid, let rest briefly on the counter until scoopable.

3. Serve scoops of ice cream generously drizzled with Dad's Hot Fudge Sauce and dolloped with *Extremely* Special Whipped Cream. Keep the ice cream, wrapped, in the freezer for up to a week.

Farm-Stand Strawberry No-Churn Ice Cream

MAKES ABOUT 2 QUARTS OF
ICE CREAM
ACTIVE TIME: 8 MINUTES
INACTIVE TIME: 4 TO 6 HOURS

1 pound (454 g) strawberries,
hulled and finely chopped

2 tablespoons freshly squeezed
lemon juice

2 tablespoons granulated sugar

One 14-ounce can (397 g) sweetened condensed milk

1 teaspoon vanilla extract

½ teaspoon kosher salt

2 cups (474 ml) heavy cream, cold

This pink-hued ice cream, studded with flecks and chunks of red berries, is for all the strawberry lovers in the house. The berries are macerated in lemon and sugar for 15 minutes to preclude them from getting icy when frozen but chopping them finely helps as well. A food processor will make easy work of such strawberry chopping (though be sure not to puree them), but if taking out your food processor makes you ballistic and scream, "I thought this was an easy baking book," skip it and go to town with a cutting board and a chef's knife.

1. Have ready a 2-quart baking dish, such as an 8-inch square baking pan or an 11-by-7-inch Pyrex® baking dish (due to the pound of strawberries called for in this recipe—you're welcome— you'll need a slightly larger vessel than the standard no-churn 8½-by-4½-inch loaf pan).

2. Combine the berries, juice, and sugar in a medium bowl and let sit for 15 minutes, stirring occasionally. Whisk together the sweetened condensed milk, vanilla, and salt in a large bowl. Whisk the heavy cream on medium to medium-high speed in the bowl of a stand mixer fitted with the whisk attachment, until stiff peaks form.

3. Stir the strawberries and any accumulated juice into the milk mixture and then gently fold in the whipped cream in two installments. Scrape the ice cream into the pan, smooth the top, and tightly cover in plastic wrap. Freeze for 4 to 6 hours, depending on how soft you like your ice cream (I'm partial to soft here, in case you were wondering). If frozen solid, let rest briefly on the counter until scoopable. The strawberries are a bit icy straight out of the gate, but perfectly soften in a matter of minutes.

4. Keep the ice cream, wrapped, in the freezer for up to a week.

Espresso Ganache Swirl No-Churn Ice Cream

MAKES 1½ QUARTS OF ICE CREAM
ACTIVE TIME: 15 MINUTES
INACTIVE TIME: 4 TO 6 HOURS

FOR THE GANACHE SWIRL
½ cup (85 g) semisweet chocolate chips
¼ cup (59 ml) heavy cream
¼ teaspoon kosher salt

FOR THE ICE CREAM
One 14-ounce can (397 g) sweetened condensed milk
1 teaspoon vanilla extract
½ teaspoon kosher salt
2 cups (474 ml) heavy cream, cold
3 tablespoons espresso powder

I'm not sure no-churn ice cream gets more heavenly than this combo of coffee and chocolate. And although I originally intended to call for store-bought hot fudge sauce in this recipe, the ganache here is so easy and so texturally perfect for swirling, that it just elevates this simplest of chilly treats into something worth writing home about (or at least texting or DMing . . .). No-churn ice cream requires whipped cream, so you will need to pull out your stand or hand mixer for this recipe—but for out-of-this-world ice cream that doesn't require an ice cream maker, I think you'll agree, it's 100 percent worth it.

1. Place an 8½-by-4½-inch metal loaf pan in the freezer.

2. To make the ganache, microwave the chips, heavy cream, and salt together in a medium, microwave-safe bowl on HIGH for two 30-second bursts, stirring after each, until melted and smooth. Let cool to room temperature on the counter, stirring periodically, while you make the ice cream base.

3. To make the ice cream, whisk together the sweetened condensed milk, vanilla, and salt in a large bowl. Whisk together the heavy cream and espresso powder on medium to medium-high speed in the bowl of a stand mixer fitted with the whisk attachment, until stiff peaks form. Gently fold the whipped cream into the milk mixture in two installments and place the bowl in the freezer to chill for about 25 minutes. This initial freezer-time helps set the ice cream so when you swirl in the ganache it stays swirly—and we're all about the swirl, am I right?

4. After 25 minutes, scrape half of the ice cream into the chilled pan, then evenly dollop half of the ganache over the top and swirl it with a paring knife. Repeat with the remaining ice cream and ganache. The pan will be quite full. Tightly cover in plastic wrap and freeze for 3½ to 5½ hours, depending on how soft you like your ice cream (I'm partial to soft here, in case you were wondering). If frozen solid, let rest briefly on the counter until scoopable. Keep the ice cream, wrapped, in the freezer for up to a week.

Oliver's Simplest Tiramisu

MAKES ABOUT 9 SERVINGS
ACTIVE TIME: 15 MINUTES
INACTIVE TIME: 4 TO 6 HOURS

2 cups (474 ml) boiling water,
  or brewed strong coffee

2 tablespoons plus 2 teaspoons
  espresso powder (omit if using
  coffee)

½ cup (118 ml) Kahlúa, or
  another coffee-flavored
  liqueur (optional, but highly
  encouraged)

1½ cups (339 g) mascarpone,
  at room temperature

1½ cups (355 ml) heavy cream

¾ cup (90 g) confectioners' sugar

¾ teaspoon kosher salt

1 tablespoon vanilla extract

7 ounces (198 g) crisp ladyfingers

Dutch-processed cocoa powder
  for dusting

My older son has loved tiramisu since he was little, when feeding a coffee-flavored dessert to a child his age was perhaps actionable. I never made it for him at home when he was growing up, but whenever we ate out, and it was on the menu, he ordered it. I would often take a bite (I hate sharing my own food but am more than happy to taste that of other's) and loved the creaminess, almost icebox cake vibe, of it, as well as the chocolate-coffee flavor combo. Moreover, recently I was tasked with making a no-bake tiramisu cheesecake for the Kitchn and am now happy to report that I am officially team-tiramisu. And so this simple streamlined version is for my Oliver, my lover of tiramisu from way back, but also for you (and, now, me).

1. Have ready an 8-inch square cake pan.

2. Whisk together the water and espresso powder in a glass measuring cup and pour it into a small, shallow bowl along with the Kahlúa, if using. Place the mascarpone in the bowl of a stand mixer and stir it a few times with a flexible spatula to loosen it. Fit the mixer with the whisk attachment and whisk in the cream, confectioners' sugar, salt, and vanilla on medium to medium-high speed until medium peaks form, scraping the bowl periodically.

3. Briefly dip about half the ladyfingers in the coffee mixture for 2 to 3 seconds, and then place the coffee-soaked fingers on the bottom of the pan, breaking them as necessary to fit snugly, until you have created a solid layer of fingers. Evenly spread half of the mascarpone whipped cream on top of the fingers, dusting with a thin layer of cocoa powder, if you so desire. Repeat with another layer of coffee-soaked fingers and the final layer of whipped cream. Cover tightly and refrigerate for 4 to 6 hours, or overnight.

4. Generously dust the top of the cake with a thick layer of cocoa powder before serving. Keep the tiramisu, wrapped, in the refrigerator for up to 3 days.

CHAPTER 6.

Sweet & Salty

Is this everyone's favorite flavor combo or what? I mean there is just something about the combo of the sweet and the salty that makes your mouth happy. Whether it's the marriage of the melted salty caramel bits and peaches in a from-scratch dump cake, the potato chips and colorful chocolate candies (such as M&M's®), in an oatmeal cookie, the butter crackers (such as Ritz®) and chocolate in an epic bark, the salty nuts and sweet jam in almond sandwich cookies *and* in an easy-peasy linzer-esque torte, or the creamy orange filling (can you say Good Humor Creamsicle Bar®?!) and crushed pretzel crust in a no-bake pie, the recipes here have you and your sweet and salty fantasies covered. And don't be afraid to play around with some of the elements in these treats: you can use colorful chocolate candies with peanuts, such as Peanut M&M's®, for the regular in the oatmeal cookies or chop up a HEATH Toffee Bar®, instead. Fill the almond sandwich cookies with the Chocolate Malted Cream Cheese Frosting (page 50) instead of the jam one. Choose a nut other than hazelnuts for the linzer torte, and a jam other than raspberry. Substitute salted peanuts for the pretzels in the fudge, and granulated sugar for the brown in the snacking cake with penuche frosting. Here's to you living your best sweet and salty life, as you (methodically) make your way through all of the tremendous tastiness in this chapter.

"Corner Store" Oatmeal Cookies

MAKES ABOUT 20 COOKIES
ACTIVE TIME: 10 MINUTES
BAKE TIME: 10 MINUTES

1 cup (130 g) all-purpose flour

1 cup (100 g) quick 1-minute oats

¾ teaspoon kosher salt

½ teaspoon baking soda

2 cups (160 g), finely crushed potato chips, such as Cape Cod, about 4 cups, precrush

½ cup (102 g) colorful chocolate candies, such as M&M's®, plus a few for pressing into the tops for your IG capture

2 tablespoons vegetable shortening

6 tablespoons (85 g) unsalted butter, melted and cooled slightly

1 cup packed (200 g) light brown sugar

2 teaspoons vanilla extract

1 large egg, cold

These are a mash-up of "everything but the kitchen sink cookies" and monster cookies (cookies that typically call for PB and oats and colorful chocolate candies, such as M&M's®— that I made about a billion times while working at Baked, back in the day). My "corner store" version is a chewy brown sugar–oatmeal cookie that scraps the PB but keeps the colorful chocolate candies, such as M&M's®, around for good measure, and calls for copious amounts of crushed potato chips (I know, brilliant). In other words, "*the* perfect sweet and salty snack food combo—but make it a cookie." And this is not my first time at the "add potato chips to your cookies" rodeo: for in my world, snacky foods and baked goods go together like nobody's business. I mean, hello—the book *is* called *Snackable Bakes* . . .

1. Heat the oven to 350°F. Line two baking sheets with parchment paper.

2. Whisk together the flour, oats, kosher salt, and baking soda in a large bowl. Whisk in 1½ cups (120 g) of the crushed chips and the candies. Whisk the shortening into the melted butter in another large bowl until the shortening melts (if there are still a few little solid bits of shortening, don't worry); whisk in the brown sugar and vanilla, and then the egg. Gently fold the dry ingredients into the wet just until the last streak of flour disappears.

3. Place the remaining crushed potato chips in a shallow bowl. Using a 2-tablespoon portion scoop, or measuring spoons, scoop the dough into balls, press a candy or two onto the top of each ball, and roll in the bowl of chips. Place on the prepared baking sheets and bake for 10 minutes, rotating and swapping the placement of the sheets at the halfway point, until lightly browned. Remove from the oven and enjoy warm. Keep the cookies in an airtight container on the counter for up to 3 days.

The Baked Beginning

I think it's worth mentioning that not only was my job as a "junior baker" at the Brooklyn bakery, Baked, my first in a professional kitchen—and really in the food industry, period (not counting the many years I spent waiting tables while pursuing a career as an actress, but that's another sidebar for another book)—but I also managed to nail the job under highly unusual circumstances. In other words: no. I was not hired via the connections I made in culinary school, 'cause I didn't go to culinary school. And I didn't start out as a manager or barista at the bakery and move my way into pastry production—I was merely a devoted customer of the bakery and, in fact, trained as a lawyer. I walked into Baked off the street and suggested I work as an unpaid (and inexperienced) apprentice or intern. I knew nothing of sweets except that I liked them and (politely) begged to be schooled. Not surprisingly, they were wary—a mom of a couple of toddlers wants to bake cookies with a bunch of recent pastry-school graduates in their 20s? Umh, yes, yes she does. Lucky for me, despite their reservations (I mean who *does* that???), they offered me 5 hours of work every Monday . . . bagging granola. Yup, it wasn't sexy and it wasn't even baking—but I was standing in a bakery while I did it, so it was at least baking adjacent. Moreover, it didn't last forever and once they saw that I was responsible and conscientious (and horrible at vacuum packing), I was taught to make some simple baked goods; such as loaf cakes, cookies, and macaroons; Baked's version of magic bars and scotcheroos; and granola (yes, the one that went into the bags that I no longer had to fill). I tell you this story not to impress you with my confidence and fearlessness, because I am actually filled right up to the brim with self-doubt and fear, as so many of us are, but because a relatively unorthodox pursuit of employment led me to a career that I adore—and one that wasn't even on my radar during those early granola-bagging days. And, well, maybe the same could happen to you. I'd tell you the moral of the story is to follow your dreams, except that I didn't really have a dream that I was following—more like a curiosity about sweets that needed a-bake-ning (sorry, couldn't resist). So, maybe I should just say be curious and open to where said curiosity leads you, even if that is outside your comfort zone and involves being taught the tools of a trade by peeps almost half your age. Yeah. Okay. I think I'll go with that.

Brown Sugar Snacking Cake with Salted Penuche Frosting

MAKES ONE 8-INCH SQUARE CAKE

ACTIVE TIME: 20 MINUTES

BAKE TIME: 25 TO 30 MINUTES

Cooking spray or softened unsalted butter for pan

FOR THE CAKE

1 cup packed (200 g) light brown sugar

½ cup (118 ml) vegetable oil

1½ teaspoons vanilla extract

2 large eggs

½ cup (118 ml) very cold tap water

1½ teaspoons baking powder

½ teaspoon kosher salt

1½ cups (195 g) all-purpose flour

FOR THE FROSTING

¼ cup (56 g) unsalted butter

½ cup packed (100 g) light brown sugar

3 tablespoons heavy cream

¾ cup (90 g) confectioners' sugar

1 teaspoon vanilla extract

½ teaspoon kosher salt

Flaky sea salt for sprinkling

This brown sugar cake has a super-soft crumb and is lightly sweetened with my beloved brown sugar. The penuche frosting (which is, for those not in the know, a brown sugar–based frosting/glaze) sets up with its telltale crust, and the combo of the plush cake and the crackly glaze is out of this world.

1. Heat the oven to 350°F. Grease an 8-inch square cake pan with cooking spray or softened butter. Line with a large piece of parchment paper that extends up and over two opposite sides of the pan.

2. To make the cake, whisk together the brown sugar, oil, and vanilla in a large bowl for 30 seconds. Whisk in the eggs, one at a time, and then the water. Sprinkle the baking powder and kosher salt into the bowl, one at a time, vigorously whisking after each. Gently fold in the flour with a flexible spatula, until most of the lumps in the batter have disappeared—a few lumps are fine.

3. Scrape the batter into the prepared pan, smooth the top, and bake for 25 to 30 minutes, rotating at the halfway point, until a wooden skewer inserted into the center comes out with a moist crumb or two. Remove from the oven and let cool in the pan for about 20 minutes, or until you can safely lift the cake out by the parchment overhang without burning yourself. Run a butter knife around the edges if it resists. Let cool to room temperature before frosting.

4. To make the frosting, cook the butter, brown sugar, and heavy cream together in a medium saucepan over medium-high heat until bubbling, stirring occasionally with a flexible spatula. Lower the heat to medium and simmer for 1 minute, stirring constantly. Remove from the heat and vigorously whisk in the confectioners' sugar, vanilla, and kosher salt, until thick and spreadable. Pour the frosting straight from the pot onto the cake and spread it over the top of the cake with a small offset spatula or butter knife (no need to frost the sides), sprinkle with flaky sea salt, and serve. Keep the cake, wrapped, on the counter for up to 3 days.

From-Scratch Peach Caramel Dump Cake

MAKES ONE 8-INCH SQUARE CAKE

ACTIVE TIME: 8 MINUTES

BAKE TIME: 48 TO 52 MINUTES

FOR THE PEACHES

¼ cup packed (50 g) light brown sugar

1 tablespoon cornstarch

½ teaspoon kosher salt

2 pounds (907 g) unpeeled peaches, fresh or frozen, cut into ½-inch slices

2 teaspoons vanilla extract

½ cup (110 g) soft caramel candies, such as Werther's, cut into ½-inch bits

FOR THE CAKE

1⅓ cups (173 g) all-purpose flour

1 cup packed (200 g) light brown sugar

1½ teaspoons baking powder

¾ teaspoon kosher salt

¾ cup (169 g) unsalted butter, sliced thinly into pats

Vanilla ice cream for serving

A "dump cake" traditionally calls for a store-bought cake mix and a can of fruity pie filling, and full disclosure: I had never even tasted a "dump cake" until developing and testing this one. But not only did I not grow up eating them, I had never even heard *mention* of them until relatively recently and I am still mad about it. This is a homemade version, so instead of canned peach pie filling, you'll use fresh (or frozen) peaches that you will not need to peel, and instead of a cake from a box, you'll make your own (insanely easy one). In fact, the caramel bits are the only store-bought component in the cake, and when they melt into the peaches, they give the cake that sweet and salty vibe we all covet.

1. Heat the oven to 375°F. Have ready an 8-inch cake pan or a 2-quart baking dish.

2. To prepare the peaches, whisk the brown sugar, cornstarch, and salt together directly in the pan. "Dump" in the peaches, sprinkle with the vanilla, and toss to coat with your hands or a flexible spatula. Evenly scatter the caramel bits over the peaches, tucking some underneath the slices, for optimal distribution.

3. To make the cake, whisk together the flour, brown sugar, baking powder, and salt in a medium bowl and evenly sprinkle the mixture over the peaches, pressing down lightly with your hands. Do not stir. Evenly distribute the butter pats over the top, layering them a bit or spacing them out a bit—whatever it takes for optimal coverage—and bake for 48 to 52 minutes, rotating at the halfway point, until the fruit is bubbling in the center when you probe the topping with a wooden skewer, as well as around the edges, and the cake is a deep, golden brown. Remove from the oven and serve warm with vanilla ice cream. Keep the cake, wrapped, on the counter or in the refrigerator for up to 3 days.

Individual Butterscotch Puddings

MAKES 6 PUDDINGS
ACTIVE TIME: 15 MINUTES
INACTIVE TIME: 2 HOURS

3 tablespoons cornstarch

1¼ teaspoons kosher salt

½ cup packed (100 g) dark brown sugar

2 cups (474 ml) whole milk

1 cup (237 ml) heavy cream

2 egg yolks

¾ cup (127 g) butterscotch chips

1 tablespoon vanilla extract

2 tablespoons unsalted butter, at room temperature

Extremely Special Whipped Cream (page 230) for serving (optional)

Butterscotch pudding might be the unsung hero of the pudding world. I mean, chocolate and vanilla—and even lemon—get all the attention, but no one ever talks about butterscotch. Or, if they do, there might be a candy thermometer involved, or a caramel that needs making, or an extended stovetop cook. Here, however, I have turned to my trusty friend the butterscotch chip to make a perfectly textured, creamy, quicker than quick, sweet and salty pud that you'll likely soon have on repeat. And I know: not everyone is on board with butterscotch chips. But even Stephanie, my former coworker from my Baked days, who tested *every* recipe in this book and is decidedly *anti*-butterscotch chips, had to admit that they are fab in this pudding. And because I love you, I really tried to develop this recipe with whole eggs, but the texture benefits immeasurably from the yolks, and so that is what you'll need to use—throw one of the whites into the Straight-Up Coconut Macaroons (page 124), and the other into Kathy's Sugar and Spice Pecans (page 147).

1. Have ready six 6-ounce ramekins or teacups.

2. Whisk together the cornstarch, salt, and brown sugar in a medium pot. Whisk in the milk and cream. Finally, whisk in the yolks. Place the pot over medium-high heat and, whisking constantly, cook until the pudding thickens and large bubbles begin sputtering on the surface, 5 to 10 minutes. Lower the heat to medium (if the sputtering is overwhelming) and let the pudding bubble, whisking constantly, for 1 minute. Remove from the heat, add the chips, vanilla, and butter, and stir until melted. Pour or ladle the pudding into the ramekins. Cover each with plastic wrap that directly touches the top of the pudding (to avoid the dreaded pudding "skin") and refrigerate until firm, about 2 hours.

3. Serve with *Extremely* Special Whipped Cream (if using). Keep the puddings, wrapped, in the refrigerator for up to 3 days.

Almond Sandwich Cookies with Jam Buttercream

MAKES 12 SANDWICH COOKIES
ACTIVE TIME: 20 MINUTES
BAKE TIME: 12 TO 15 MINUTES

FOR THE BUTTERCREAM
⅓ cup plus 2 tablespoons (131 g) jam (your choice)
½ cup (113 g) unsalted butter, at room temperature
1 teaspoon almond extract, or to taste
¼ teaspoon vanilla extract
½ teaspoon kosher salt
2 cups (240 g) confectioners' sugar
2 to 3 tablespoons heavy cream, at room temperature

FOR THE COOKIES
1 cup (200 g) granulated sugar
¼ cup (59 ml) vegetable oil
¼ teaspoon vanilla extract
½ teaspoon almond extract, or to taste
1 large egg
¼ cup (56 g) sour cream
2 teaspoons baking powder
½ teaspoon kosher salt
½ cup (51 g) almond flour
1½ cups (195 g) all-purpose flour

A handful of sliced almonds for decorating (optional)

These endearing little almond-jam numbers are adorable and delicious, but they do take a hot minute to assemble, so please don't hold it against me. Briefly boiling the jam in the microwave before adding it to the buttercream, thickens it, and makes the filling a little sturdier (thanks, Dorie Greenspan, for the tip).

1. Heat the oven to 350°F. Line two baking sheets with parchment paper.

2. To prepare the jam for the buttercream, microwave it in a small, microwave-safe bowl for two or three 30 second-bursts, stirring after each, until the jam is bubbling all over. Let cool while you assemble the cookies and buttercream.

3. To make the cookies, whisk together the granulated sugar, oil, and extracts in a large bowl for 30 seconds. Whisk in the egg and then the sour cream. Sprinkle the baking powder and salt into the bowl, one at a time, vigorously whisking after each. Whisk in the almond flour; then gently fold in the all-purpose flour with a flexible spatula, just until the last streak disappears.

4. Scoop 1½ tablespoons of batter, using a portion scoop or measuring spoons, and evenly place 12 on each prepared baking sheet. Place an almond slice (if using) on the top of half of the cookies. Bake for 12 to 15 minutes, rotating and swapping the placement of the sheets at the halfway point, until the cookies are dry to the touch and crackly topped. Remove from the oven and let cool to room temperature on the pans before filling.

5. To make the buttercream, beat together the butter, extracts, and salt on medium-low speed in the bowl of a stand mixer fitted with the paddle attachment, until smooth. Beat in the confectioners' sugar, ½ cup (60 g) at a time, alternating with splashes of the cream, scraping the bowl with a flexible spatula, as needed. Beat on medium speed for an additional 3 minutes, or until light and fluffy. Remove the bowl and fold in 2 tablespoons of the jam with a flexible spatula.

6. Turn the cooled cookies *without* the almond slices upside down and evenly spread 1 teaspoon of the remaining jam on top of each one. Top the jam with about 1½ tablespoons of buttercream and cover with an upturned, almond-studded cookie, pressing gently. Refrigerate for 30 minutes. Keep the sandwich cookies in an airtight container on the counter or in the refrigerator for up to 3 days.

Simple Lattice(less) Linzer Torte

MAKES ONE 8-INCH ROUND "TORTE"
ACTIVE TIME: 15 MINUTES
BAKE TIME: 40 TO 45 MINUTES

Cooking spray or softened unsalted butter for pan
1½ cups (195 g) all-purpose flour
1 cup (107 g) hazelnut flour
¼ cup (36 g) skinless hazelnuts, roughly chopped (toasting is nice, but not necessary)
⅔ cup (133 g) granulated sugar
½ teaspoon baking powder
¾ teaspoon kosher salt
1 teaspoon ground cinnamon
½ cup (113 g) unsalted butter, cold and cubed
1 large egg, cold
½ teaspoon vanilla extract
¾ cup (214 g) raspberry jam
Confectioners' sugar for dusting

Now, don't get me wrong: linzer tortes do indeed appeal to the laid-back baker in me, as they are filled with store-bought preserves and their nutty dough is simple to prepare and serves as both the torte's bottom and its latticed top. But a *latticed* top has no place in a snackable bake book, am I right? So, inspired by the dessert queen, Alice Medrich, I have kept all that I value most about linzers (the tasty, easy, press-in dough and the jar of jam from the grocery) but have removed the lattice, crumbling the extra dough on top of the torte instead. Genius, I know (thanks, Alice). Use the left-over hazelnut flour to make Hazelnut Chip Snacking Cake (page 136); or, if you want to make your own, see page 14. And if you can't find skinless hazelnuts, see page 119 for how to skin your own.

1. Heat the oven to 350°F. Generously grease an 8-inch round cake pan with cooking spray or softened butter. Line the bottom with parchment paper.

2. To make the topping and crust, whisk together the flours, nuts, granulated sugar, baking powder, salt, and cinnamon in a medium bowl. Rub the butter into the dry ingredients, using your fingers, until the butter is crumbly and pea-sized. Add the egg and vanilla and stir them into the crumbly mixture using a fork, or your hands, until the dough holds together when squeezed. You can do all of this in a food processor, if that feels uncomplicated to you. Refrigerate 1 cup (180 g), about one-third, of the dough in a small bowl. Evenly press what remains onto the bottom of the prepared pan. Spread with the jam, leaving a little border. Crumble the reserved dough and evenly scatter it over the jam. Bake for 40 to 45 minutes, rotating at the halfway point, until the topping is nicely browned and the jam is bubbling.

3. Remove from the oven and let rest for about 10 minutes, then run a butter knife around the edge of the pan to loosen the torte, as the jam has a tendency to stick as it cools. Let the torte come to room temperature in the pan and then invert it onto a serving plate, right side up. Dust with confectioners' sugar, slice, and serve. Keep the torte, wrapped, on the counter for up to 3 days.

No-Bake Orange Cream Pie with a Pretzel Crust

MAKES ONE 9-INCH ROUND PIE
ACTIVE TIME: 20 MINUTES
INACTIVE TIME: 4 TO 6 HOURS

Cooking spray or softened
  unsalted butter for pan

FOR THE CRUST

1½ cups (150 g) finely ground pretzel crumbs (from about 3 cups
  whole pretzels)

¼ cup packed (50 g) light brown
  sugar

½ teaspoon kosher salt

10 tablespoons (141 g) unsalted
  butter, melted and cooled
  slightly

FOR THE FILLING

1 cup (237 ml) heavy cream

8 ounces (226 g) cream cheese,
  at room temperature

1¼ cups (150 g) confectioners'
  sugar

2 tablespoons orange zest

1 teaspoon vanilla extract

1 tablespoon freshly squeezed
  lemon juice

½ cup (118 ml) defrosted orange
  juice concentrate

Extremely Special Whipped
  Cream (page 230) for serving

Who knew that an orange cream pie would end up being one of my most prized snackable bakes? Not me, that's for darn sure. I mean I loved the *idea* of a creamy, orange pie filling, reminiscent of a Good Humor Creamsicle® bar, with a salty crust made from pretzels, but I wasn't sure what to expect when developing the recipe. And I am thus so pleased to share that it is all that, and then some. The sweet citrus "Creamsicle-esque" filling is marvelous with the salty pretzel crust (and if you've never made a pretzel crust before, wow, you are in for a treat). The secret ingredient here is orange juice concentrate, as it provides just the right amount of orange flavor without loosening the filling. Please make yourself some OJ with the extra concentrate. Also, you will need a food processer here for the luscious citrus filling, as sometimes a girl's just gotta process, but I'm betting you could use a stand mixer on low speed, in a pinch.

1. Grease a 9-inch pie plate with cooking spray or softened butter.

2. To make the crust, process the pretzels, brown sugar, and salt together in the bowl of a food processor until the pretzels are finely ground. Some small pretzel bits are fine, as you don't want just pretzel dust. Pour in the melted butter and process until the mixture holds together when squeezed. Alternatively, you may place the dry ingredients in a resealable plastic bag, seal and cover it with a tea towel, and crush the pretzels with a rolling pin, then transfer the crumbs to a medium bowl and stir in the melted butter. Scrape the crust mixture into the prepared pie plate, firmly press it into the bottom and up the sides with your fingers or the bottom of a 1-cup dry measuring cup, and freeze while you make the filling.

3. To make the filling, give the processor bowl and blade a quick rinse or wipe down, and process the cream until thick—it won't exactly have peaks, the way it does when you whisk it in a stand mixer, but it will stand upright if encouraged to do so. Transfer the thickened cream to a large bowl. If your kitchen is warm, place it in the refrigerator.

4. Without cleaning the bowl, process the cream cheese, confectioners' sugar, zest, vanilla, and lemon juice until thick and smooth. Add the concentrate and process until incorporated. Gently fold the orange mixture into the whipped cream in two installments with a flexible spatula. Don't overmix.

5. Scrape the filling into the crust, smooth the top, cover with plastic wrap, and refrigerate for 4 to 6 hours, or overnight. If the crust sticks to the pie plate, when you attempt to cut your first slice, rub the bottom and sides of the plate with a wet tea towel dampened with hot water. Serve slices with a dollop of *Extremely* Special Whipped Cream. Keep the pie, wrapped, in the refrigerator for up to 3 days.

Salty-Snack Chocolate Fudge with Pretzels and Crushed Potato Chips

MAKES 36 LARGE PIECES
OR 64 TINY ONES
ACTIVE TIME: 5 MINUTES
INACTIVE TIME: 2 HOURS

Cooking spray or softened
unsalted butter for pan

2⅔ cups (454 g) semisweet chocolate chips

One 14-ounce can (397 g) sweetened condensed milk

2 teaspoons vanilla extract

1 teaspoon kosher salt

2 cups (160 g) crushed potato
chips, such as Cape Cod,
about 4 cups precrush

1¾ cups (131 g) crushed pretzels
(from about 2⅔ cups whole
pretzels)

Flaky sea salt for sprinkling

Turbinado sugar for sprinkling

Typically, homemade fudge can be a tad tricky to get right, requiring not only a thermometer and some rigorous stirring, but some inherent candy-making skills, as well, so as to achieve a creamy texture, as opposed to a gritty one. And so—big surprise—I've never been all that excited about making it from scratch. Just too nit-picky for my fuss-free self. But a few years back, I was introduced to the wonder that is *sweetened condensed milk* fudge and I am now—above all else—an enthusiastic convert. Not only does the fudge take about five minutes to assemble, but it is literally IMPOSSIBLE to screw up (my kind of snackable treat). Here, I have packed the fudge full of potato chips (Cape Cod for life, FYI) and pretzels, guaranteeing that each and every bite is a literal sweet, salty, and *crunchy* explosion in your mouth.

1. Grease an 8-inch square cake pan with cooking spray or softened butter. Line with a long sheet of parchment paper that extends up and over two opposite sides of the pan.

2. Microwave the chocolate and sweetened condensed milk on HIGH in a large, microwave-safe bowl in two 45-second bursts, stirring after each with a flexible spatula, until the chocolate melts. Stir in the vanilla and kosher salt, and then the chips and pretzels. Scrape the fudge into the prepared pan. Drape with a sheet of parchment paper and flatten with your hands. Sprinkle with flaky sea salt and turbinado sugar.

3. Refrigerate until firm, about 2 hours, and slice with a chef's knife. Keep the fudge in an airtight container on the counter for up to 1 week.

Butter Cracker Toffee Bark with Toasted Nuts

MAKES ABOUT 2 POUNDS
OF BARK

ACTIVE TIME: 12 MINUTES

BAKE TIME: 10 TO 12 MINUTES

64 butter crackers (220 g), such
as Ritz® (about 2 sleeves)

2 cups packed (200 g) light
brown sugar

1 cup (226 g) unsalted butter

2 teaspoons vanilla extract

1½ teaspoons kosher salt

1¼ cups (213 g) semisweet chocolate chips

1 cup (112 g) deeply toasted nuts,
such as pecans, walnuts, or
almonds, finely chopped

Flaky sea salt for sprinkling

Ritz® Crackers are just the best crackers. That's all I have to say. And if you've never made "bark" with butter crackers before, get ready for your mind to be blown. You do you here when it comes to choosing the chocolate and the nuts, but I'm partial to semisweet and pecans, in case you were wondering. And no matter the nut you choose, deeply toasting is key, for the most flavorful and crunchy texture. See page 17 for how to do so.

1. Heat the oven to 350°F. Line a baking sheet with aluminum foil. No need to grease it.

2. Place the crackers on the prepared sheet, overlapping them a little in places, so that they all fit. Bring the brown sugar and butter to a boil in a medium saucepan over medium-high heat. Lower the heat to medium and, whisking constantly, cook until it thickens into a toffee, about 3 minutes. Off the heat, whisk in the vanilla and kosher salt, pour the toffee over the crackers, and spread it into an even layer with an offset spatula, or the back of a spoon, carefully adjusting any crackers that get dislodged. Bake until the toffee bubbles and darkens slightly, 10 to 12 minutes. Remove from the oven and immediately sprinkle with the chocolate chips. Let the chips begin to soften and melt, about 5 minutes, and then spread them over the toffee. Sprinkle with the nuts and flaky sea salt and refrigerate until chilled, about 1 hour, or freeze for 25 to 30 minutes. Break into pieces and serve.

3. Keep the bark in an airtight container on the counter or in the refrigerator for up to a week.

Sweet & Salty Caramel Popcorn

MAKES 10 CUPS OF POPCORN
ACTIVE TIME: 10 MINUTES
BAKE TIME: 1 HOUR

Cooking spray or softened
   unsalted butter for pan
10 cups (100 g) popped popcorn, unsalted (from ½ cup
   unpopped kernels, if popping
   your own)
1½ cups (200 g) roasted and
   salted peanuts
1 cup (200 g) light brown sugar
¼ cup (80 g) light corn syrup
1 tablespoon molasses
½ cup (113 g) unsalted butter
1 teaspoon kosher salt
½ teaspoon baking soda
2 teaspoons vanilla extract

Being somewhat indifferent to sports—a position of which I am not proud, but if you cannot tell the truth in your own baking book, then where *can* you tell the truth?—the affection with which I remember Red Sox games at Fenway Park with my dad and brother growing up, seems misplaced and somewhat peculiar. But like so many fondly recalled events from my childhood, it is in fact *the food served at the park* that I remember so romantically and with such devotion. And although I love a hot dog as much as the next gal, Cracker Jack® popcorn made me love baseball like nothing else could. I loved the box and the prize, natch, but I truly loved the combo of the sweet, caramelized corn and the salty peanuts the most. Cracker Jack® popcorn is just straight-up the bomb, in my opinion. And if you've never made caramel popcorn at home, guess what? Not only is the homemade stuff one of life's great sweet and salty treats, but it is not hard, I promise—you don't even need a candy thermometer. I like the peanuts here, as they provide that true Jacks-from-a-box vibe, but it's totes okay to leave them out. And as for the popcorn, you can buy it already popped (preferably unsalted), use unsalted microwave popcorn (my preference), or pop your own on the stovetop.

1. Heat the oven to 250°F. Have ready a baking sheet lined with parchment paper that you have secured to the four corners of the pan with a little cooking spray or softened butter.

2. Evenly spread the popped popcorn on the prepared baking sheet and sprinkle with the peanuts. Bring the brown sugar, corn syrup, molasses, and butter to a boil over medium heat in a medium pot, stirring occasionally with a flexible spatula. Let boil for about 5 minutes, without stirring, until the caramel is thick and fragrant. Off the heat, stir in the salt, baking soda, and vanilla. Working quickly, pour the caramel over the popcorn and stir to coat. Bake the popcorn for an hour, stirring it every 15 minutes to ensure even baking.

3. Remove from the oven and let cool to room temperature on the pan. Transfer the popcorn to a big bowl, hide some prizes among the kernels, and enjoy. Keep the popcorn in an airtight container on the counter for up to a week.

Hazelnut Brittle with Chocolate Drizzle

MAKES ABOUT 2½ POUNDS
OF BRITTLE
ACTIVE TIME: 20 MINUTES
INACTIVE TIME: 20 MINUTES
TO AN HOUR

Cooking spray or softened
　unsalted butter for pan
2 tablespoons unsalted butter
2 teaspoons baking soda
2 teaspoons kosher salt
2 teaspoons vanilla extract
2½ cups (332 g) deeply toasted
　hazelnuts, skinless, coarsely
　chopped
2 cups (400 g) granulated sugar
⅔ cup (220 g) light corn syrup
1 cup (237 ml) water
3 tablespoons semisweet choco-
　late chips
Flaky sea salt for sprinkling

Caramel + hazelnuts + chocolate = salty, nutty, sweet excel-
lence; and so, umh . . . duh: this brittle is undeniably delectable.
But move quickly when assembling it, my dears! Brittle requires
speed, so make sure you have ALL your ingredients ready and
by your side when you begin, so that as soon as your sugar
begins to darken, you are ready to go. If you can only find hazelnuts with skins, see page 119 for how to remove them.

1. Have ready a baking sheet lined with parchment paper that you
    have secured to the four corners of the pan with a little cook-
    ing spray or softened butter. Also, have the butter, baking soda,
    salt, vanilla, and nuts measured out and ready to go.

2. Bring the sugar, corn syrup, and water to a boil in a medium
    pot over high heat. Cook without stirring until the mixture just
    turns a light amber color, 14 to 15 minutes. As it begins to color,
    you can swirl the pot a bit by moving it gently with potholder-
    protected hands but resist the urge to stir. Off the heat, quickly
    stir in the butter, and then the baking soda, kosher salt, and
    vanilla, and finally the nuts, with a flexible spatula. Pour the
    mixture onto the prepared baking sheet and spread it as thinly
    as you can, about ¼ inch thick or thinner. The brittle is *very* hot
    so be careful. Sprinkle with flaky sea salt and bring to room tem-
    perature by freezing for 20 minutes or cooling on the counter for
    an hour.

3. Microwave 1½ tablespoons of the chips on HIGH in a small,
    microwave-safe bowl in two 15-second bursts, stirring after
    each with a spoon. Add the unmelted chips to the melted ones
    and stir until all the chips are melted (this is a little "temper-
    ing" hack [thank you, Stephanie!] and will keep your chocolate
    drizzle from melting all over your fingers while you break and
    eat your brittle). Drizzle the chocolate over the cooled brittle by
    dipping the spoon in the chocolate and gently waving it over the
    brittle.

4. Let the chocolate set briefly before cracking the brittle into
    pieces and serving. Keep the brittle in an airtight container on
    the counter for up to 3 weeks.

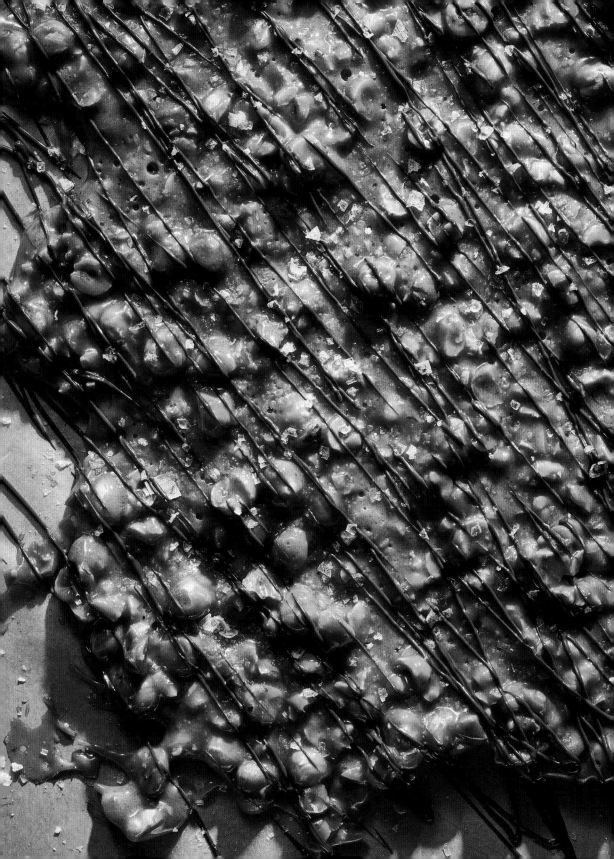

CHAPTER 7.

A Little Zippy & a Little Zesty

Although I'm not the gal with the *largest* of spice collections or a steady rotation of fresh herbs in the fridge or garden, I get it that certain bakes benefit immeasurably from a little zhuzhing. So, in this chapter, we've got a little spiciness happening—Mexican Hot Chocolate Pudding Cake (page 217) and Double Ginger Scones with Currants (page 198), for example—and some herbaceous vibes, too—such as Thyme Nectarine Fools (page 214) and Strawberry Basil Crumb Bars (page 206). But, as you've come to expect, every last one of these snackable bakes is a breeze to assemble, as the spices called for are all likely available where you shop (and you probably already have some of them at home—hello, cinnamon), as are the herbs, like basil and thyme. Now I get it that you might not have dried culinary lavender in the cupboard for the Tiny Lavender Shortbread Bites (page 205), so apologies in advance, but you can easily find it online—or omit it (the bites will still be the easiest and tastiest you've ever had—hyperbolic, but true). Moreover, just gotta say: *please* make my Chocolate Gingerbread Snacking Cake with Tangy Crème Fraîche Whipped Cream (page 222) even if you *think* gingerbread just isn't your thing (it's not mine either, FYI), and please whip up a batch of my Epic Snickerdoodles for Stephanie (page 209), too. Stephanie tested all the recipes in this book and is a mad baking genius and *loves* snickerdoodles—so bake them with her in mind. Don't get me wrong, if I've said it once, I've said it, well, a lot: I love *all* my bakes, but since I've got your attention (hi!), just wanted to flag those two. Okay, enough said. Have at it. Enjoy. Spices and herbs for the win, and all that.

Double Ginger Scones with Currants

MAKES 7 JUMBO SCONES
ACTIVE TIME: 8 MINUTES
BAKE TIME: 22 TO 27 MINUTES

FOR THE SCONES
2 cups (260 g) all-purpose flour
½ cup packed (100 g) light brown sugar
1 tablespoon baking powder
1 teaspoon ground ginger
1 teaspoon kosher salt
10 tablespoons (141 g) unsalted butter, cold and cubed
½ cup (75 g) dried currants or raisins
½ cup (80 g) crystallized ginger, coarsely chopped
½ cup (118 ml) heavy cream, cold
1½ teaspoons vanilla extract
1 large egg, cold

FOR THE EGG WASH
1 large egg
¼ teaspoon kosher salt

Turbinado sugar for sprinkling

These took a hot minute to make perfect, but perfect they are. I was hoping to include chopped pears in the mix, inspired by the Pear Ginger Raisin Scones at the now shuttered Once Upon a Tart in SoHo. But the pears made the scones too wet, and when I replaced them with crystallized ginger, a spicy star was born. I scoop these—to portion them—with a big ole portion scoop (we did it this way at Baked), so there's no fussy kneading on a floured work surface, rolling out, and cutting happening here. If you can't find currants, or are (weirdly) anti-currant, you can substitute raisins.

1. Heat the oven to 375°F. Line a baking sheet with parchment paper.

2. To make the scones, whisk together the flour, brown sugar, baking powder, ginger, and salt in a large bowl. Rub the butter into the flour mixture with your fingers until the butter is crumbly and pea-sized. Add the currants and crystallized ginger and toss to combine. Whisk together the cream, vanilla, and egg in a 2-cup glass measuring cup and pour over the dry ingredients. Gently stir with a flexible spatula until the loose bits of flour just disappear.

3. Divide the dough into 7 balls (about ½ cup each) with a portion scoop or a ½-cup dry measure, and evenly place them on the prepared baking sheet. The dough will be sticky.

4. To make the egg wash, whisk together the egg and salt in a small bowl and brush onto the scones. Sprinkle the scones with the turbinado sugar.

5. Bake for 22 to 27 minutes, rotating at the halfway point, until the scones are nicely browned and a wooden skewer inserted into the center of one comes out clean. Remove from the oven and let them cool on the pan for about 5 minutes before serving.

6. The scones are best the day they are made but will keep in an airtight container on the counter for up to 3 days.

Cinnamon-Sugar Buttermilk Donut Holes

MAKES 30 DONUT HOLES
ACTIVE TIME: 20 MINUTES
BAKE TIME: 8 TO 10 MINUTES

Cooking spray or softened
   unsalted butter for pan

FOR THE DONUTS
6 tablespoons (85 g) unsalted
   butter, melted and cooled
   slightly
½ cup packed (100 g) light brown
   sugar
1 teaspoon vanilla extract
1 large egg
½ cup (118 ml) buttermilk
½ teaspoon baking powder
¼ teaspoon baking soda
½ teaspoon kosher salt
1 teaspoon freshly grated
   nutmeg
1½ cups (195 g) all-purpose flour

FOR THE CINNAMON-SUGAR
½ cup (113 g) unsalted butter,
   melted
¾ cup (150 g) granulated sugar
2¼ teaspoons ground cinnamon

These donut holes are really just mini, nutmeg-infused muffins that are drenched in melted butter when still warm, rolled in cinnamon-sugar, and then popped in your mouth one after the other. They are perfect for breakfast (obvs) but also make for a fantastically fun and retro dinner party dessert.

———

1. Heat the oven to 350°F. Generously grease a 24-well mini muffin tin with cooking spray or softened butter.

2. To make the donuts, whisk together the butter, brown sugar, and vanilla in a large bowl for 30 seconds. Whisk in the egg and then the buttermilk. Sprinkle the baking powder, baking soda, salt, and nutmeg into the bowl, one at a time, vigorously whisking after each. Gently fold in the flour with a flexible spatula just until the last streak disappears. Fill each prepared mini well with 1 tablespoon of batter, using either a small portion scoop or a measuring spoon.

3. Bake for 8 to 10 minutes, rotating the pan at the halfway point. The donuts are done when their tops look dry, they bounce back after being lightly pressed, and a wooden skewer inserted into the center of one comes out clean or with a moist crumb or two.

4. While they bake, make the cinnamon-sugar coating by pouring the melted butter in one small bowl and whisking together the granulated sugar and cinnamon in another. Place a cooling rack over a baking sheet.

5. Remove the donuts from the oven and, as soon as you can safely handle them without burning yourself, dunk each donut into the butter, lifting it out with a slotted spoon, and then rolling it in the cinnamon-sugar, using a large fork or your hands to nudge it around, before transferring it to the cooling rack.

6. Bake off the remaining batter, rinsing the pan in cold water to cool it, drying, and re-greasing it between rounds and, once baked, dunk and roll the remaining donuts. Enjoy warm or at room temperature. Keep the donuts in an airtight container on the counter for up to 3 days.

Flourless Salt & Pepper Chocolate Cookies

MAKES 18 COOKIES
ACTIVE TIME: 5 MINUTES
BAKE TIME: 12 MINUTES

1¼ cups plus 1 tablespoon (157 g) confectioners' sugar

¼ cup plus 2 tablespoons (30 g) Dutch-processed cocoa powder

3 tablespoons cornstarch

½ teaspoon kosher salt

¾ teaspoon freshly ground black pepper, or to taste

2 large egg whites, at room temperature

2 teaspoons vanilla extract

½ cup (85 g) semisweet chocolate chips

Flaky sea salt and freshly ground black pepper for sprinkling

Inspired by Payard's famous Flourless Chocolate Walnut Cookies, as well as Baked's Salt and Pepper Sandwich Cookies, these are fudgy, chewy (due to a little cornstarch), a little spicy, and *flourless* (you're welcome). They don't call for any nuts, but they do call for chips and you'll need them for structure (this is a loose-battered cookie, if ever there was one). Use the leftover yolks in the Individual Butterscotch Puddings (page 180) and please make ice cream sandwiches with these cookies and the Espresso Ganache-Swirl No-Churn Ice Cream (page 167), and then call me.

1. Heat the oven to 325°F. Line two baking sheets with parchment paper.

2. Whisk together the confectioners' sugar, cocoa powder, cornstarch, kosher salt, and pepper in a large bowl. Fold in the egg whites and vanilla and then the chocolate chips with a flexible spatula just until incorporated. If you overmix the whites, the cookies do not bake properly. The batter will be very runny. Using a 1-tablespoon portion scoop or measuring spoon, portion out the batter onto the prepared baking sheets, nine cookies per sheet, leaving plenty of room between them, as they will spread. Sprinkle each one with a little flaky sea salt and pepper and bake for 12 minutes, rotating and swapping the placement of the sheets at the halfway point.

3. The cookies are ready when they look shiny and cracked. Remove from the oven and let the cookies cool to room temperature on the baking sheets before removing them, either by gently peeling away the paper with your fingers, or by using a spatula. Keep the cookies in an airtight container on the counter for up to 3 days.

Tiny Lavender Shortbread Bites

MAKES 36 TRIANGULAR BITES
ACTIVE TIME: 5 MINUTES
BAKE TIME: 30 MINUTES

Cooking spray or softened
    unsalted butter for pan
¾ cup (90 g) confectioners' sugar
1 cup (226 g) unsalted butter,
    melted and cooled slightly
1 tablespoon plus 1 teaspoon
    culinary-grade lavender buds,
    roughly chopped
½ teaspoon kosher sea salt
2 cups (260 g) all-purpose flour
1 tablespoon granulated sugar

I think the world of a sweets shortcut and am forever seeking them out. So, when I discovered one could make the most-buttery of shortbreads with melted butter, in about 2 minutes in a single bowl with a whisk and a spatula, of course I had to give it a go. The results are these tiny lavender bites: lightly floral, but not perfume-y, buttery for days, and crumbly and tender in all the best shortbread ways. . . . Wait a minute. Did you catch what I did there? With the rhyme? Totally unintentional, but cute, no? Anyway, omit the lavender if you'd rather not track it down (though you should be able to find it at Whole Foods, online, and at most health food stores).

1. Heat the oven to 350°F. Grease an 8-inch square cake pan with cooking spray or softened butter. Line with a long sheet of parchment paper that extends up and over two opposite sides of the pan.

2. Whisk together the confectioners' sugar and butter in a large bowl. Sprinkle 1 tablespoon of the lavender and the salt into the bowl, one at a time, vigorously whisking after each. Gently fold in the flour with a flexible spatula just until the last streak disappears. Scrape the dough into the prepared pan and press it into the bottom with your hands. Rub the remaining teaspoon of lavender into the granulated sugar in a small bowl and sprinkle over the shortbread.

3. Bake for 30 minutes, rotating at the halfway point, until lightly browned. Remove from the oven and immediately slice the shortbread, still in the pan, into 16 squares, using a sharp paring knife. Then slice each square in half diagonally to make 32 tiny triangles. Once cooled to room temperature, lift the shortbread from the pan with the parchment overhang. Run a butter knife around the edges if it resists. Keep the shortbread in an airtight container on the counter for up to 3 days.

Strawberry Basil Crumb Bars

MAKES 16 BARS
ACTIVE TIME: 12 MINUTES
BAKE TIME: 50 TO 55 MINUTES

Cooking spray or softened
   unsalted butter for pan

FOR THE FILLING

1 to 2 tablespoons finely
   chopped basil (from 5 to 10
   leaves), plus more for garnish

⅓ cup (67 g) granulated sugar, or
   more/less depending on the
   sweetness of your berries

2 teaspoons cornstarch

2½ cups (350 g) hulled and
   roughly chopped strawberries, about 1-inch pieces

2 teaspoons freshly squeezed
   lemon juice

FOR THE CRUST AND CRUMB

1 cup (130 g) all-purpose flour

1 cup (100 g) quick 1-minute oats

¾ teaspoon kosher salt

¾ cup (150 g) granulated sugar

10 tablespoons (142 g) unsalted
   butter, cold and cubed

1 teaspoon vanilla extract

I love the combo of strawberries and basil. Especially here, where the basil is rubbed into the sugar and then tossed with the berries, giving the bars a subtle earthy, springlike dimension, rather than a straight-up, "yum, basil" vibe. But leave it out if the earth and the spring are not your things, or if you just like your strawberry flavor unadulterated. The buttery crust and crumb are made from the same dough and run a little soft and tender, as opposed to crispy.

1. Heat the oven to 375°F. Grease an 8-inch square cake pan with cooking spray or softened butter. Line with a long sheet of parchment paper that extends up and over two opposite sides of the pan.

2. Begin the filling: Rub the basil into the sugar with your fingers in a medium bowl. Whisk in the cornstarch and set aside while you prepare the crust and crumb.

3. To make the crust and crumb, whisk together the flour, oats, salt, and sugar in a large bowl. Rub the butter into the flour mixture with your fingers until the butter is pea-sized. Stir in the vanilla and, using a large fork, continue to mix until the dough holds together when squeezed. Press two-thirds of the dough firmly into the prepared pan.

4. Complete the filling: Toss the strawberries in the basil sugar along with the lemon juice, and scatter them over the dough. Crumble the reserved dough and cover the berries with it. Bake the bars for 50 to 60 minutes, rotating the pan at the halfway point, until the topping is browned and the strawberries are bubbling in the center.

5. Remove from the oven, let cool briefly on the counter, 5 to 10 minutes, and then run a butter knife around the edges to release any sticky bits, and cool completely. Run a knife around the edges once more and lift the bars out of the pan by the parchment overhang. Sprinkle with finely chopped basil, slice, and serve. Keep the bars in an airtight container in the refrigerator for up to 3 days.

Epic Snickerdoodles for Stephanie

MAKES ABOUT 20 COOKIES
ACTIVE TIME: 10 MINUTES
BAKE TIME: 6 TO 8 MINUTES

FOR THE COOKIES

3 tablespoons vegetable shortening

5 tablespoons (71 g) unsalted butter, almost melted, but with a few soft but solid pieces remaining

¾ cup packed (150 g) light brown sugar

1 teaspoon vanilla extract

1 large egg, cold

½ teaspoon baking soda

½ teaspoon kosher salt

¼ teaspoon ground cinnamon

1 teaspoon cream of tartar

1½ cups (195 g) all-purpose flour

FOR THE CINNAMON-SUGAR

3 tablespoons granulated sugar

1½ teaspoons ground cinnamon

Snickerdoodles are my recipe tester Steph's most coveted cookie and maybe now mine, too. These are 'doodles of the slightly puffy variety, and they are soft middled, crispy edged, and delish. I do go out on a bit of a limb here, and call for adding brown sugar, vanilla, and cinnamon to the cookie dough—none of which is traditional, but all of which you'll be into, so don't worry. Please melt your butter *only* until most of it has melted; see page 17 for a little how-to. A few soft, remaining butter chunks ensure it will cool quickly, and cool butter = cool dough = cookies that don't spread. Finally, a short bake time at a high temp is the snickerdoodle badge of honor, so don't be tempted to go long and low. Neither Steph, nor I, will be happy if you do.

1. Heat the oven to 375°F. Line two baking sheets with parchment paper.

2. To make the cookies, whisk the shortening into the warm butter in a large bowl until the shortening melts (if there are still a few little solid bits of shortening, don't worry). Whisk in the brown sugar and vanilla for 30 seconds, and then the egg. Sprinkle the baking soda, salt, cinnamon, and cream of tartar into the bowl, one at a time, vigorously whisking after each. Gently fold in the flour with a flexible spatula just until the last streak disappears. Don't overmix.

3. To make the cinnamon-sugar, whisk together the granulated sugar and cinnamon in a small bowl. Scoop 1½-tablespoon balls of dough with a portion scoop or measuring spoons and drop them in the cinnamon-sugar, nudging them with your fingers to coat. Place 9 or 10 on each prepared baking sheet. The dough is super soft. Don't worry. Bake for 6 to 8 minutes, until the cookies are cracked and slightly domed (they may or may not collapse as they cool—depends on the temp in your kitchen). Remove from the oven and if too domed/puffy for your liking, immediately press with a spatula to flatten. Enjoy warm or at room temperature. Keep the snickerdoodles in an airtight container on the counter for up to 3 days.

Banana Whoopie Pies with Chai Cream Cheese Filling

MAKES 16 WHOOPIE PIES
ACTIVE TIME: 20 MINUTES
BAKE TIME: 8 TO 10 MINUTES

FOR THE WHOOPIES

1 cup packed (200 g) light brown sugar

¼ cup plus 2 tablespoons (88 ml) vegetable oil

1 teaspoon vanilla extract

1 large egg

¾ cup (172 g) mashed bananas (from about 1½ medium very ripe bananas)

¾ teaspoon baking powder

½ teaspoon baking soda

½ teaspoon kosher salt

½ teaspoon ground cinnamon

2 cups (260 g) all-purpose flour

FOR THE FILLING

6 tablespoons (85 g) unsalted butter, at room temperature

6 ounces (170 g) cream cheese, at room temperature

2¼ teaspoons vanilla extract

½ teaspoon kosher salt

¾ teaspoon ground cinnamon

¾ teaspoon ground cardamom

⅛ teaspoon ground ginger

⅛ teaspoon freshly grated nutmeg

1½ cups (180 g) confectioners' sugar

I can't exactly explain why, but the combo of fruity, mildly sweet bananas and warm and toasty chai spices (folded into a cream cheese filling, no less) is a literal "chef's kiss" kind of situation. Yes, the filling will require you to pull out a few more spices than one usually grabs when snackable baking, but I wouldn't ask you to do so if it wasn't worth it. And despite requiring two components (pies + filling), this bake is still not a big deal to throw together, in case you were getting anxious and thinking otherwise.

1. Heat the oven to 350°F. Line two baking sheets with parchment paper.

2. To make the whoopies, whisk together the brown sugar, oil, and vanilla in a large bowl for 30 seconds. Whisk in the egg and then the bananas. Sprinkle the baking powder, baking soda, salt, and cinnamon into the bowl, one at a time, vigorously whisking after each. Gently fold in the flour with a flexible spatula just until the last streak disappears. Don't overmix.

3. Scoop 1½ tablespoons of batter, using a portion scoop or measuring spoons, evenly placing 12 on each prepared baking sheet. Bake for 8 to 10 minutes, rotating and swapping the placement of the sheets at the halfway point, until the pies are dry to the touch and bounce back when lightly pressed. Remove from the oven and let cool to room temperature on the pans before filling. Repeat with any remaining batter.

4. To make the filling, beat together the butter and cream cheese on medium-low in the bowl of a stand mixer fitted with the paddle attachment, just until combined. Beat in the vanilla, salt, and spices and then, gradually, the confectioners' sugar. Beat for an additional 30 seconds on medium speed.

5. Turn half of the pies upside down, top with about 1½ tablespoons of filling, and cover with an upturned pie, pressing gently. Refrigerate for 30 minutes to set (they're arguably tastier when chilled). Keep the whoopies in an airtight container in the refrigerator for up to 3 days.

VARIATION

For Banana Whoopie Pies
with Chocolate Malted Cream
Cheese Filling, replace the
chai filling with a double
batch of Chocolate Malted
Cream Cheese Frosting
(page 50).

Red Velvet Loaf Cake with Cinnamon Cream Cheese Glaze

MAKES ONE 8½-BY-4½-INCH
LOAF CAKE

ACTIVE TIME: 15 MINUTES
BAKE TIME: 50 TO 55 MINUTES

Cooking spray or softened
  unsalted butter for pan

FOR THE CAKE
1 cup (237 ml) vegetable oil

1 cup (200 g) granulated sugar

½ teaspoon vanilla extract

2 large eggs, at room
  temperature

⅔ cup (158 ml) buttermilk, at room
  temperature

1½ teaspoons red food coloring (if
  you dig a brighter red, add up
  to ¼ to ½ teaspoon more)

1¼ teaspoons white vinegar

¾ teaspoon baking soda

2½ tablespoons Dutch-processed
  cocoa powder

¾ teaspoon kosher salt

1⅔ cups (217 g) all-purpose flour

FOR THE GLAZE
3 ounces (85 g) cream cheese,
  at room temperature

½ cup (60 g) confectioners' sugar

½ teaspoon ground cinnamon

⅛ teaspoon kosher salt

2 tablespoons buttermilk

½ teaspoon vanilla extract

I've always had a soft spot for red velvet cake. I mean if you dig chocolate cake and you're okay with food coloring, what's not to like? But the red velvet layer cake at Cake Man Raven, a bakery near my first home in Brooklyn, turned me into a devotee. The cake was so moist, tender, and so chocolaty, and, well, red, that it was nothing short of irresistible. This glazed loaf is my snackable version of Cake Man's cake, and not only is it easier to assemble than a layered, frosted situation, but it is equally as fab-looking (and tasting) in its own understated way.

1. Preheat the oven to 350°F. Grease an 8½-by-4½-inch loaf pan with cooking spray or softened butter. Line the bottom with a long sheet of parchment paper that extends up and over the two long sides of the pan (like a cradle for your cake).

2. To make the cake, whisk together the oil, granulated sugar, and vanilla in a large bowl for 30 seconds. Whisk in the eggs, then the buttermilk, the food coloring, and the vinegar. Sprinkle the baking soda, cocoa powder, and salt into the bowl, one at a time, vigorously whisking after each. Gently fold in the flour with a flexible spatula, just until some, but not all, of the lumps disappear. Scrape the batter into the prepared pan, smooth the top, and bake for 50 to 55 minutes, rotating at the halfway point. The cake is done when a wooden skewer inserted into the center comes out with a moist crumb or two.

3. Remove from the oven and let cool in the pan for about 20 minutes, or until you can safely lift the cake out by the parchment overhang without burning yourself. Run a butter knife around the edges if it resists. Let cool to room temperature before glazing.

4. To make the glaze, gently whisk together the cream cheese, confectioners' sugar, cinnamon, and salt in a medium bowl until combined, then vigorously whisk until smooth. Whisk in the buttermilk and vanilla and pour decoratively over the top of the cooled cake. You will have leftover glaze. Refrigerate for about 15 minutes to set the glaze before serving with extra glaze on the side. Keep the cake, wrapped, in the refrigerator for up to 3 days.

Thyme Nectarine Fools

MAKES 6 INDIVIDUAL FOOLS
ACTIVE TIME: 10 MINUTES
INACTIVE TIME: 2 HOURS

1 tablespoon plus 1 teaspoon
    fresh thyme, chopped, plus a
    few sprigs for garnish

3 tablespoons granulated sugar

2 cups (280 g) finely chopped
    nectarines (no need to peel
    them; about 4 small nectar-
    ines), plus more for garnish

1 teaspoon freshly squeezed
    lemon juice

1½ cups (355 ml) heavy cream

¼ cup (30 g) confectioners' sugar

1½ teaspoons vanilla extract

18 (154 g) shortbread cookies,
    such as Pepperidge Farm
    Chessmen

A fool is a creamy dessert of luscious whipped cream, studded with juicy fruit, and layered with softened cookies. And if you're fond of effortless sweets and treats (which you must be if you've got this book in your hands), then I think it's fair to say that you're going to dig the occasional fool. Here, chopped nectarines and thyme-infused sugar (it sounds fancier and more complicated than it is, I promise) are crushed together, folded into thyme whipped cream, and layered with cookies. Briefly chilled to soften the cookies, the resulting fools will give you all the summer feels, not to mention the perfect-simple-dessert ones.

---

1. Have ready six 6-ounce glasses.

2. Rub 1 tablespoon of thyme into the granulated sugar with your fingers in a medium bowl. Stir in the nectarines and lemon juice and press down on them with a slotted spoon, crushing them just a bit so they release some of their juice.

3. Whisk together the cream, confectioners' sugar, vanilla, and the remaining teaspoon of thyme on medium to medium-high speed in the bowl of a stand mixer fitted with the whisk attachment, until medium peaks form. Gently fold the nectarines into the cream.

4. Crush a cookie into the bottom of each of the six glasses and dollop about ¼ cup of nectarine cream on top. Repeat twice more, evenly dividing any remaining cream among the six glasses. Garnish each with a slice of nectarine and sprig of thyme. Serve immediately or refrigerate until the cookies soften, about 2 hours. Keep the fools, wrapped, in the refrigerator for up to 3 days.

Mexican Hot Chocolate Pudding Cake

MAKES ONE 8-INCH SQUARE CAKE

ACTIVE TIME: 7 MINUTES

BAKE TIME: 30 MINUTES

FOR THE BOTTOM LAYER

6 tablespoons (85 g) unsalted butter, melted

1 cup packed (200 g) light brown sugar

2 teaspoons vanilla extract

½ cup (118 ml) whole milk

⅓ cup (27 g) Dutch-processed cocoa powder

2 teaspoons baking powder

1¼ teaspoons ground cinnamon

A rounded ¼ teaspoon chile powder, such as cayenne pepper, or to taste

½ teaspoon kosher salt

1 cup (130 g) all-purpose flour

FOR THE TOP LAYER

¼ cup (20 g) Dutch-processed cocoa powder

½ cup packed (100 g) light brown sugar

1¼ cups very hot tap water

2 teaspoons espresso powder (optional)

⅓ cup (57 g) semisweet chocolate chips, for sprinkling

A drizzle of heavy cream or vanilla ice cream for serving

Some people call pudding cakes "chocolate cobblers" or "self-saucing" cakes, but I just call them friggin' deeeelish and pretty magical. After quickly assembling and scraping a simple spiced chocolate cake batter into a pan, a warm chocolate concoction is poured over it and the whole shebang is baked until the bottom turns to hot fudge and the top to a rich, steamed chocolate cake. As the cake rests postbake, the hot fudge layer thickens into pudding and then the fun really begins, as each serving is both cake plus chocolate sauce—and with a drizzle of cream or a scoop of ice cream, there's no question you'll be living your best and scrummiest (as the Brits say) snackable-bake life.

1. Heat the oven to 350°F. Have ready an 8-inch square cake pan.

2. To make the bottom layer, whisk together the butter, brown sugar, and vanilla in a large bowl. Whisk in the milk. Sprinkle the cocoa powder, baking powder, cinnamon, chile powder, and salt into the bowl, one at a time, vigorously whisking after each. Fold in the flour with a flexible spatula just until the last streak disappears. Scrape the batter into the pan.

3. To make the top layer, using the same bowl (no need to clean it), whisk together the cocoa powder, brown sugar, water, and espresso powder (if using). Pour this mixture over the batter in the pan, but do not mix them together. Sprinkle with the chips. Bake for about 30 minutes, rotating at the halfway point. The cake is done when it still looks slightly soft and underbaked in the middle, but drier and cakelike around the edges, and when you shimmy the pan on the oven rack (with a potholder-clad hand!), the middle of the cake jiggles. Remove from the oven and let the cake rest at least 15 minutes if you want a fudgy, saucelike bottom layer and 30 minutes for a more puddinglike experience. Both are spectacular, FYI. Serve warm, straight from the pan with a drizzle of heavy cream or a scoop of vanilla ice cream. Keep the cake, wrapped, on the counter for up to 3 days.

Spiced Pumpkin Snacking Cake with Fluffiest Chocolate Buttercream

MAKES ONE 8-INCH SQUARE CAKE

ACTIVE TIME: 20 MINUTES

BAKE TIME: 27 TO 30 MINUTES

Cooking spray or softened unsalted butter for pan

FOR THE CAKE

1½ cups (195 g) all-purpose flour

1 teaspoon baking powder

⅛ teaspoon baking soda

½ teaspoon kosher salt

1 teaspoon ground cinnamon

½ teaspoon freshly grated nutmeg

¼ teaspoon ground ginger

½ cup (118 g) vegetable oil

1¼ cups (250 g) granulated sugar

1 teaspoon vanilla extract

2 large eggs

A scant 1 cup (213 g) pure pumpkin puree, half of a 15-ounce can

FOR THE BUTTERCREAM

½ cup (113 g) unsalted butter, at room temperature

1¼ cups (150 g) confectioners' sugar

⅓ cup (27 g) Dutch-processed cocoa powder

¼ teaspoon kosher salt

2 tablespoons whole milk

1½ teaspoons vanilla extract

This cake turned me into a pumpkin lover. Yes, you're right: that is partly due to the fact it is paired with (an outstanding) chocolate buttercream, and chocolate is always a wildly influential player. But there is something else going on here, too. The warming spices, the bright orange color (the fact that it's a *snacking* cake), the tight soft crumb, and the way the flavor and texture improve over a few days, all contribute to making it one of my go-to fall faves. And the cake easily doubles if you're feeling sheety. And I hope it goes without saying, that if you're just not up for pulling out your stand mixer for the frosting, glaze this cutie with the Chocolate Glaze on page 85 instead.

1. Heat the oven to 350°F. Grease an 8-inch square cake pan with cooking spray or softened butter. Line with a long piece of parchment paper that extends up the two opposite sides of the pan.

2. To make the cake, whisk together the flour, baking powder, baking soda, salt, cinnamon, nutmeg, and ginger in a medium bowl. Whisk together the oil, granulated sugar, and vanilla in a large bowl for 30 seconds; whisk in the eggs, one at a time, and then the pumpkin. Gently fold the dry ingredients into the wet with a flexible spatula just until the last streak of flour disappears. If the batter is super lumpy, give it a few more folds until most of the lumps disappear. Scrape the batter into the prepared pan and shimmy the pan on the counter to even out the batter.

3. Bake for 27 to 30 minutes, rotating at the halfway point, until a wooden skewer inserted into the center comes out with a moist crumb or two. Remove from the oven and let cool in the pan for about 20 minutes, or until you can safely lift the cake out by the parchment overhang without burning yourself. Run a butter knife around the edges if it resists. Let cool to room temperature before frosting.

4. To make the buttercream, beat the butter on medium-low speed in the bowl of a stand mixer fitted with the paddle attachment until smooth. Beat in the confectioners' sugar, a little at a time, and then the cocoa powder and salt, until combined, scraping the bowl with a flexible spatula, as needed. Beat in the milk and vanilla and continue to beat on medium speed for an additional 3 to 5 minutes, as the frosting lightens in color and gets fluffier. Generously frost the cake, leaving the sides bare, and serve. Keep the cake, wrapped, on the counter for up to 3 days.

VARIATION

For Spiced Pumpkin Snacking Cake with Cinnamon Cream Cheese Frosting, substitute Cinnamon Cream Cheese Frosting (page 221) for the Fluffiest Chocolate Buttercream.

Nonnie's Best-Ever Carrot Cupcakes with Cinnamon Cream Cheese Frosting

MAKES 12 CUPCAKES
ACTIVE TIME: 20 MINUTES
BAKE TIME: 18 TO 20 MINUTES

FOR THE CUPCAKES

1 cup (200 g) granulated sugar
½ cup (118 g) vegetable oil
1 teaspoon vanilla extract
2 large eggs
1 teaspoon baking powder
¼ teaspoon baking soda
1 teaspoon ground cinnamon
¼ teaspoon kosher salt
1 cup (130 g) all-purpose flour
1⅓ cups lightly packed (127 g) finely grated carrots (about 2 medium carrots)
½ cup (40 g) sweetened shredded coconut

FOR THE FROSTING

6 tablespoons (85 g) unsalted butter, at room temperature
6 ounces (170 g) cream cheese, at room temperature
2¼ teaspoons vanilla extract
½ teaspoon kosher salt
¾ teaspoon ground cinnamon
1½ cups (180 g) confectioners' sugar
Ground cinnamon for dusting

My mother-in-law's carrot cake is the stuff of legends. It is a moist, sweet, slightly spiced layer cake, with some sweetened shredded coconut folded in for good measure, and a thick, finger-licking-good, tangy cream cheese frosting. Her recipe is so legendary, in fact, that it is an internet darling (not sure who originally shared it with Nonnie, all those many decades ago, but they clearly shared it with a few others, as well). I've tweaked it a little here, but if it looks familiar, neither Nonnie, nor I, is surprised. We also won't be surprised if you'd rather glaze these little numbers with the Cream Cheese Glaze (page 80) rather than pull out your stand mixer for the frosting.

1. Heat the oven to 350°F. Line a 12-well muffin tin with paper liners.

2. To make the cupcakes, whisk together the granulated sugar, oil, and vanilla in a large bowl for 30 seconds. Whisk in the eggs, one at a time. Sprinkle the baking powder, baking soda, cinnamon, and salt into the bowl, one at a time, vigorously whisking after each. Gently fold in the flour with a flexible spatula just until a few streaks of flour remain. Fold in the carrots and coconut. Fill each prepared muffin well about three-quarters full, using a ¼-cup portion scoop or measuring cup, and bake for 18 to 20 minutes, rotating at the halfway point, until a wooden skewer inserted into the center of one of the cups comes out with a moist crumb or two. Remove from the oven and let cool for about 5 minutes, or until you can safely remove the cupcakes from the tin without burning yourself. Let cool to room temperature before frosting.

3. To make the frosting, beat together the butter and cream cheese on medium-low speed in the bowl of a stand mixer fitted with the paddle attachment, just until combined. Beat in the vanilla, salt, and cinnamon and then, gradually, the confectioners' sugar. Beat for an additional 30 seconds on medium speed. Decoratively spread each cupcake with about 2 tablespoons of frosting. Dust cinnamon over each and place in the refrigerator for 15 minutes to firm up before serving. Keep the cupcakes in an airtight container in the refrigerator for up to 3 days.

Chocolate Gingerbread Snacking Cake with Tangy Crème Fraîche Whipped Cream

MAKES ONE 8-INCH SQUARE CAKE

ACTIVE TIME: 15 MINUTES

BAKE TIME: 25 TO 30 MINUTES

Cooking spray or softened unsalted butter for pan

FOR THE CAKE

⅓ cup (79 ml) vegetable oil

⅔ cup packed (133 g) dark or light brown sugar

⅓ cup (27 g) Dutch-processed cocoa powder, plus more for dusting

½ cup (118 g) unsulfured molasses

1 teaspoon vanilla extract

½ teaspoon baking soda

¾ teaspoon espresso powder (optional)

⅓ cup (79 ml) very hot tap water

1 large egg

⅔ cup (87 g) all-purpose flour

¾ teaspoon kosher salt

2 teaspoons ground ginger

¾ teaspoon ground cinnamon

⅛ teaspoon ground white pepper, or freshly ground black

FOR THE WHIPPED CREAM

½ cup (115 g) crème fraîche, at room temperature

1 cup (237 ml) heavy cream

1 teaspoon vanilla extract

⅓ cup (40 g) confectioners' sugar

Although I am not 100-percent team gingerbread cake, I am 1,000-percent team *chocolate* gingerbread cake. Inspired by the chocolate-ginger Bundt we used to make at Baked, this easy, spicy, slightly "damp" (a Nigella word, if you can't tell), and richly chocolaty cake is truly superb; and this is despite the fact that she's a tad sunken in her center. However, if I've said it once (which I have), looks are overrated. Moreover, topped with swoops and swirls of the most *divine* crème fraîche whipped cream, no one will be the wiser—and a slightly sunken center means extra whipped cream on those sunken middle slices, which means *yum*.

---

1. Heat the oven to 325°F. Grease an 8-inch square cake pan with cooking spray or softened butter. Line with a long sheet of parchment paper that extends up and over two opposite sides of the pan.

2. To make the cake, whisk together the oil, brown sugar, cocoa powder, molasses, vanilla, baking soda, espresso powder (if using), and water in a large bowl for 30 seconds. Whisk in the egg, and then the flour, salt, ginger, cinnamon, and pepper until smooth. Pour the batter into the prepared pan and gently tap the pan on the counter a few times to release any air bubbles.

3. Bake for 25 to 30 minutes, rotating at the halfway point, until a wooden skewer inserted into the center comes out clean, or with a moist crumb or two. The top center may look a little "damp" and a tiny bit sunken, and that is a-okay. Remove from the oven and let cool in the pan until room temperature, then lift the cake out by the parchment overhang. Run a butter knife around the edges if it resists.

4. To make the whipped cream, whisk together all its ingredients on medium to medium-high speed in the bowl of a stand mixer fitted with the whisk attachment, until soft peaks form. Generously spread over the cake (the sunken center makes for an excellent whipped cream "cradle"), dust with cocoa powder, and serve. Keep the cake, wrapped, in the refrigerator for up to 3 days.

Mini Apple Cardamom Crumbles

MAKES 6 INDIVIDUAL
CRUMBLES
ACTIVE TIME: 8 MINUTES
BAKE TIME: 25 TO 30 MINUTES

FOR THE APPLES

¼ cup (50 g) granulated sugar

2 teaspoons cornstarch

1 teaspoon ground cardamom

½ teaspoon kosher salt

3 large apples (about 2 pounds;
907 g), such as Granny Smith,
peeled, cored, and cut into
½-inch wedges

1 tablespoon freshly squeezed
lemon juice

FOR THE CRUMBLE

¾ cup (97 g) all-purpose flour

¼ cup (25 g) quick 1-minute oats

1 cup packed (200 g) light brown
sugar

⅛ teaspoon kosher salt

1 teaspoon ground cardamom

½ cup (113 g) unsalted butter, cold
and cubed

Heavy cream for drizzling

I'm not usually a lover of oats in my crumble topping, but something about the combo of cardamom and oats inspired me to include them here, and I have to say, I'm super into it. A little spicy, a little sweet, and very autumnal, these darlings pay homage to my mom's (legendary) apple brown betty (which was really just an apple crisp—but don't tell *her*). These minis are *generously* crumble covered, thank you very much, 'cause life is just better topped with more buttery, sugary (and oaty!) bits. But those sneaky crumbly bits definitely sink as the apples bake and collapse—and you will definitely see that happen after you pull them from the oven, so just take a deep breath, and then dig in.

1. Heat the oven to 350°F. Place six 6-ounce heatproof ramekins on a baking sheet (if you use larger ramekins, you will need to make fewer crumbles).

2. To prepare the apples, whisk together the granulated sugar, cornstarch, cardamom, and salt in a large bowl. Toss the apples and lemon juice in the mixture with a flexible spatula, then evenly divide them among the six ramekins.

3. To make the crumble, whisk together the flour, oats, brown sugar, salt, and cardamom in the same bowl in which you just prepared the apples (no need to clean it first). Rub the butter into the dry ingredients with your fingers until the mixture holds together when squeezed. Generously sprinkle the crumble evenly over the apples, pressing it so it adheres and in order to achieve maximum crumble coverage. Bake for 25 to 30 minutes, until the crumble is lightly browned and the apples are bubbling underneath it in the center (you can check by poking at it a bit with a wooden skewer). Remove from the oven and let cool about 15 minutes before serving with a drizzle of heavy cream. Keep the crumbles, wrapped, on the counter for up to 3 days.

Jack's Next-Level Cinnamon-Sugar Toast

MAKES 4 SLICES OF TOAST
ACTIVE TIME: 5 MINUTES
BROIL TIME: 3 TO 5 MINUTES

Vegetable oil for brushing

4 slices challah or brioche, about ¾ inch thick

¼ cup packed (50 g) light brown sugar

¾ teaspoon ground cinnamon

½ teaspoon kosher salt

A pinch of freshly grated nutmeg, or to taste

4 tablespoons (56 g) unsalted butter, at room temperature

½ teaspoon vanilla extract

My younger son, Jack, was raised on cinnamon toast, as all the best young men are. Here, I've created a "next-level" toast for him that he (thankfully) heartily approves of (he has a notoriously discerning palate, so if he likes it, it's safe to say we all will). The bread here is fried before being broiled because fried is my favorite food group—and because fried toast = perfect toast (oh, and feel free to elevate the fry with olive oil—not sure what Jack will say, but I'm into it). And once broiled, the buttery cinnamon-sugar topping caramelizes in just about the dreamiest of ways possible. Ordinary cinnamon-sugar toast, eat your heart out.

1. Line a toaster oven tray, if you have one, or a baking sheet, with aluminum foil.

2. Heat a large skillet over medium to medium-high heat. Handling the bread gently, as it can be soft and tear easily, lightly brush both sides of each slice with oil and then grill each side in the hot pan, until golden brown, 1 to 2 minutes per side. If all the bread cannot fit in the pan at the same time, grill two slices at a time. Remove from the pan and let cool while you make the topping.

3. Whisk together the brown sugar, cinnamon, salt, and nutmeg in a small bowl. Smoosh (technical baking term, peeps) in the butter and vanilla with a fork. Evenly divide the mixture among the four bread slices, spreading each thickly. If using a toaster oven, place the slices on the prepared tray and broil the tops until the cinnamon-sugar topping caramelizes and bubbles, about 5 minutes. If using a regular oven, adjust the top rack, so that the toast won't be super close to the broiler, place the slices on the prepared baking sheet, and broil until the cinnamon-sugar topping caramelizes and bubbles, 3 to 5 minutes, watching carefully, as the edges have a tendency to singe. Remove from the oven and serve immediately.

CHAPTER 8.

A Couple of Easy-Peasy Toppings

Whipped cream makes everything better. That is just a stone-cold fact. It makes slices of pie, scoops of ice cream, fruit crumbles, a bowl of berries—you name it—*better.* And I hope this is a safe space, because I've got an admission: I've been known to eat a particularly flavorful one, like the salted honey one from my Salted Honey Ginger Icebox Cake (page 153), and the lemon one from my Lemon Pucker Shortbread Icebox Cake (page 157) straight-up with a spoon. But my *Extremely* Special Whipped Cream is really something, well, extremely special because it is *stabilized* whipped cream, which means it will last up to a week (if not longer) in the refrigerator. And if there is anything better than straight-up whipped cream, it is whipped cream that sticks around for a few days. Oh, and the hot fudge here is that of which all your hot fudge dreams are made, in case you were wondering—chewy, fudgy, deeply chocolaty (what with both Dutch-processed cocoa powder *and* chocolate chips), and supremely silky and smooth—and will be utterly excellent on any of the ice creams herein.

Extremely Special Whipped Cream

MAKES ABOUT 2 CUPS (227 G)
ACTIVE TIME: 5 MINUTES

1 regular-sized marshmallow, or
    15 minis, or 1 generous table-
    spoon of marshmallow crème
1 cup (237 ml) heavy cream, cold
1 tablespoon confectioners'
    sugar
1 teaspoon vanilla extract

This is a whipped cream game changer, because, believe it or not, if you add a tablespoon of marshmallow crème (such as Fluff) or a handful of melted mini marshies (or a single regular-sized one) to your heavy cream when whipped cream–making, the resultant cream lasts for up to a week, no joke. If you happen to have all three on hand (that would be me), the marshmallow crème is the most user-friendly, as you don't need to melt it—and it's vegetarian, to boot. Word to the wise: stale marshies, won't melt, so be sure yours are fresh.

——————

Microwave the regular-sized marshmallow or minis (if using the crème, no need to microwave it first) in a small, microwave-safe bowl until melted, about two 5-second bursts on HIGH. Scrape it into the bowl of a stand mixer fitted with the whisk attachment. Add the cream, confectioners' sugar, and vanilla and whisk on medium to medium-high speed until medium peaks form. Transfer to an airtight container and refrigerate for up to a week (okay, longer—I don't think I'm allowed to say that, but it's true).

Dad's Hot Fudge Sauce

MAKES ABOUT 2½ CUPS
(592 ML) HOT FUDGE SAUCE

ACTIVE TIME: 5 MINUTES

INACTIVE TIME: 15 TO 20
MINUTES

¾ cup (177 ml) heavy cream

½ cup (160 g) light corn syrup

¼ cup (30 g) confectioners' sugar

¼ cup (20 g) Dutch-processed
cocoa powder

1¼ cups (210 g) semisweet chocolate chips

3 tablespoons unsalted butter

2 teaspoons vanilla extract

¾ teaspoon kosher salt

This sauce is thick, fudgy, chocolaty, and chewy (yes, *chewy*, as any fudge sauce worth its weight in ice cream is). And although I call it "Dad's," my father has never whipped up a jar of hot fudge sauce in his entire life (although he used to be quite skilled at Toll House cookies, roast chicken, and French toast). Instead, I refer to this homemade version of vanilla ice cream's best friend as "Dad's" because all my childhood sundae-eating memories include my dad. In fact, my father and I ate more sundaes together when I was growing up than I can even recall. And no, we did not share them, but instead, we sat side by side at the counter—he with his pralines-n-cream ice cream with butterscotch sauce and me with my Peppermint Stick (page 163) ice cream with hot fudge—and just sundae'd it up in tandem. When making from-scratch fudge sauce, a little rest after it's assembled is nice. It not only intensifies the chew, but it cools the sauce a bit, so it is not so screaming hot when it hits the ice cream that it melts it, and instead remains thick and fudgy as it dribbles luxuriously down your scoop.

1. Combine the cream, corn syrup, confectioners' sugar, and cocoa powder in a small pot and bring to a boil over medium-high heat, whisking occasionally. Lower the heat to medium, whisk in the chips, and cook until they have melted, whisking constantly. Off the heat, stir in the butter, vanilla, and salt. Let sit so the sauce can thicken and develop its characteristic chew, 15 to 20 minutes. Serve over ice cream or straight-up into your mouth with a spoon.

2. Keep the sauce in a covered, heatproof container (that you can place in a microwave to reheat later) in the refrigerator for up to a month. Reheat in a microwave on HIGH in 20-second bursts, stirring after each, until liquefied.

Acknowledgments

Oh, gosh, peeps. I'm not even sure where to begin, as I am so grateful to so many (including the universe, if you must know).

I want to thank my agent, Judy Linden, who has tirelessly championed me and the cause that is easy-peasy baking. Her unyielding faith in all that I do is the kind a girl can only dream of—and she is a fantastic lunch date, to boot. My editor at Countryman Press, Ann Triestman, deserves so many thanks, not only for her enthusiastic appreciation of all things sweet and snackable, but also for her sharp editorial eye. Ann and I first met over the phone in the pre-Zoom days, when Judy and I were looking to publish *The Vintage Baker*, and I liked her no-nonsense style immediately. Thus, to my mind, it was nothing short of kismet (and the genius that is snackable baking) that brought us together five years later. Stephanie Whitten, my longtime pal from my Baked days, tested every recipe in this book—sometimes multiple times—and without her exquisite eye; discerning palate (a palate *way* more sophisticated than my own); and excellent baking, editorial, organizational, and even math skills, I would have been lost and this book would have been a whole lot less snackable. So much gratitude, Steph, truly.

Thanks, also, to my extraordinary photo team: I mean, wow. Nico Schinco, Kaitlin Wayne, and Charlotte Havelange are not only uber-creative talents, they are the absolute loveliest of humans. The two weeks that we spent shooting this book were quite literally two of the best ever. I love them so much and, when I think of all three of them, I am filled to the brim with all the grateful feels.

My beloved friend Shilpa Uskokovic was not only the person who first suggested I ask Nico about photographing *Snackable Bakes,* and who spent several days helping out during the photo shoot, but she is also the one I texted and DMed on the regular for book advice (from "Will we need to wear masks at the shoot?" to "Do you like this font?" to "You left your shoes at the studio"). No one is smarter, savvier, or more skilled in the kitchen and I am so grateful for her friendship. Thank you to Stephanie Loo, too, who not only helped out during the shoot, but also tested all of the recipe variations in the book, as well as others. Not everyone who cold emails you inquiring about work is an absolute gem and a major talent who then becomes a straight-up pal, but Stephanie is all that and then some.

And to Allison Chi, for designing the most perfect book (ever); to Jessica Gilo, for being an early *Snackable Bakes* advocate (prior to Countryman even making an offer) and for her marketing and PR wizardry; to Isabel McCarthy, for all the essential behind-the-scenes maneuvering; and to Iris Bass, for carefully and smartly tightening up my manuscript.

Thanks to my on-set hand models: my forever-fave Jessica Bacchus, and Katie's fab boyfriend, Nik McLeod. To Andrea Loret de Mola, for assisting us all with all things studio-related; to Dan and Julie Resnick, for letting us shoot in their epic Brooklyn space; and to my friend Jake Cohen, who first suggested the space might be available (and is totally responsible for my foray into Tik-Tok—insert emoji of woman shrugging, followed by a red heart emoji). Thanks to those who tested the (bafflingly tricky) Blackberry Lemon Yogurt Loaf Cake: Jenny, Theresa, Lisa, and Sally; and to Veronica, for the jumbo muffin testing. And to my blurbers—Helen, Tara, Sohui, Vallery, Zoe, Sam, and Erin—your words mean so much. As well as to Olga, Hannah, and Liza at Postcard PR—I am so pleased to have you along for the *Snackable Bakes* ride. Thanks to Amy Treadwell, for being the smartest of sounding boards when *Snackable Bakes* was in her infancy. Thanks also to every single one of my friends, and basically anyone and everyone who has ever said something nice about me and/or my easy-peasy baking, but especially to Miro, Becky, and Caroline, for all the love, support, and much-appreciated gripe sessions.

Finally, thanks to Oliver and Jack, for being mine: you two are my everything.

Index

***Boldface** indicates illustrations